ABOUT THE AUTHOR

While a 1982–86 Visiting Fellow at Harvard University, R. Hans Hilgermann synthesized his 20 years of university and corporate teaching and research into a new system for helping managers define and reach their professional goals: Goal Management. As president of the Boston-based Corporate Health–Cost Research Alliance and its Wellness Councils of Greater Boston, he applies this system to showing corporations and their managers how to reach their health goals.

Before coming to Harvard, he was director of the Speed Reading and Time Management Programs at Northwestern University, where he authored *Reading as Problem Solving*. He has also been a contributing editor for the Boston Computer Society magazine, *BCS Update*. His consulting clients have included AT&T, American Can Corp., G. D. Searle & Co., W. R. Grace & Co., First National Bank of Chicago, Hanover Insurance, and the president of Boston University. He has developed major training systems in speed reading, problem solving, time management, health promotion, and goal management.

ABOUT
IRWIN PROFESSIONAL
PUBLISHING

Irwin Professional Publishing is the nation's premier publisher of business books. As a Times Mirror company, we work closely with Times Mirror training organizations, including Zenger-Miller, Inc., Learning International, Inc., and Kaset International, to serve the training needs of business and industry.

About the Business Skills Express Series

This expanding series of authoritative, concise, and fast-paced books delivers high-quality training on key business topics at a remarkably affordable cost. The series will help managers, supervisors and frontline personnel in organizations of all sizes and types hone their business skills while enhancing job performance and career satisfaction.

Business Skills Express books are ideal for employee seminars, independent self-study, on-the-job training, and classroom-based instruction. Express books are also convenient references at work.

CONTENTS

Self-Assessment

Analyze your strengths and weaknesses as a manager of goals. There are no right or wrong answers now and we'll be reviewing these statements often. For now, just enjoy the possibilities that come to mind. Read each statement and mark the appropriate space.

	Almost Always	Sometimes	Almost Never
1. I can recite from memory my three top goals.	_____	_____	_____
2. I know what my most important needs are.	_____	_____	_____
3. Every time I complete a difficult task, I reward myself.	_____	_____	_____
4. I pursue goals for which I am not properly prepared.	_____	_____	_____
5. I have daily routines for each major goal.	_____	_____	_____
6. When I have important projects, I write a project plan.	_____	_____	_____
7. Establishing new work habits is easy for me.	_____	_____	_____
8. I consider myself a good manager of time.	_____	_____	_____
9. I regularly do things to reduce my stress.	_____	_____	_____
10. I set realistic goals for myself.	_____	_____	_____
11. When I begin a skill or habit, I measure my progress.	_____	_____	_____
12. I use success words when I talk to myself.	_____	_____	_____
13. I use success words when I talk to other people.	_____	_____	_____
14. I plan my work each day on paper.	_____	_____	_____
15. My work and home spaces are well organized.	_____	_____	_____
16. I can easily find what I need in the office files.	_____	_____	_____
17. My friends and family actively support my goals.	_____	_____	_____
18. The people I work with support my goals.	_____	_____	_____

19. I exercise vigorously three times a
     week.   _____   _____   _____

20. I feel that I am getting what I want
     out of life.   _____   _____   _____

Total   _____   _____   _____

Combined total   _____

1

What Is Goal Management?

This chapter will help you to:

- Identify your strengths and weaknesses as a goal manager.
- Discover and clarify the needs driving your goals.
- Understand the key principles of goal management.

ARE YOU A GOAL MANAGER?

Has your department missed performance targets? Are the results of the company's recent restructuring disappointing? Are your dreams of career advancement slipping out of reach?

You may need a strong dose of goal management. To find out, analyze your strengths and weaknesses as a manager of goals. Turn back to the Self-Assessment and calculate your score:

- For every check of *Almost Always*, give yourself two points.
- For every check of *Sometimes*, give yourself one point.
- For every check of *Almost Never*, give yourself no points.

Add up each column for your total score. What does your score mean? The highest possible score is 40; the lowest is 0. *40–31 points:* You're an excellent goal manager and will be an expert when you finish this book. *30–21 points:* You're doing a lot of things right and are on your way to becoming an excellent goal manager. *20–11 points:* You occasionally try goal management, but need new skills and daily habits for your goals to succeed. Whatever your score, it should be higher by the time you complete this book. This chapter explores just what goals are, what drives them, and what it means to manage them.

WHY DO YOU HAVE GOALS?

goal (*n*) the end to which a person aims to reach or accomplish; or the end to which a design tends.

In daily life, a goal is more than *an intention* to reach an end. In practical terms, a goal cannot be reached unless it is planned and the plan executed. A goal has two parts: the end result and the means of reaching it. But why do we define and pursue goals? Very simply, because we want or need something. Thus, a **goal** requires an action plan to meet a need through a series of tasks. Systematic **goal management** provides the planning, persistence, and self-discipline to complete these tasks.

Defining clear, realistic, motivating goals is the first step to successful goal management. Without clearly defined goals, you can waste time acting without purpose or pursuing the wrong goals. The first step in defining goals is determining your needs.

WHAT ARE YOUR NEEDS?

Are you motivated enough to start—and complete—a major goal? Unless you have a strong desire to complete a goal, it will never be more than an unfulfilled wish.

We rarely pursue goals for their own sakes. Goals meet needs. So, needs are the primary motivators of goals for individuals and business.

Well-defined goals always focus on meeting very specific needs. In order to define motivating goals, you must study your needs carefully. According to psychologist, Abraham Maslow, everyone shares five types, or levels, of needs: (1) physical needs, (2) security needs, (3) caring relationships needs, (4) self-worth needs, and (5) dream-realization needs. We put our energies first into meeting our physical and security needs; then we devote our resources to satisfying the other types of needs. To help you identify your needs, here is a review of the five types of needs we all have.

Physical Needs

Your needs for food, shelter, clothing, and good health will always come first. Any goal that addresses these needs will motivate you.

Security needs and dream-realization needs occupy a lot of our waking time

List unmet physical needs to be addressed:

_____   _____
_____   _____
_____   _____
_____   _____

Security Needs

Making the mortgage, rent, or car payments keeps your world orderly and secure. Keeping or improving the job that enables you to make these payments is the foundation of security. This income also purchases many of the things you require to meet your physical needs. Although money does not take care of everything, it does solve many problems that can make life difficult and distract you from important goals.

List unmet security needs to be addressed:

_____   _____
_____   _____
_____   _____
_____   _____

Caring-Relationships Needs

We tend to seek caring relationships early in our lives and then focus on a career. The result can be loneliness and alienation.

List unmet caring-relationship needs to be addressed:

_____   _____
_____   _____
_____   _____
_____   _____

Self-Worth Needs

You have strong needs to feel good about yourself and have others look up to you. Friends and close coworkers usually fill these needs. To attain your goals, you might need to find new friends and coworkers who will motivate you rather than encouraging inaction. Surround yourself with people who affirm your goals and help you reach them. Beware of those who feel threatened by your future success or your ambitions.

List your unmet self-worth needs to be addressed:

_____   _____
_____   _____
_____   _____
_____   _____

Dream-Realization Needs

Retirement is usually when people say, "Now I'm going to do all those things I couldn't do when I was working and raising a family." This is the statement of a person who mistakenly thinks that personal growth and living one's dreams are incompatible with job security and meeting responsibilities. Successful professionals often say that their jobs do not seem like work because they are having such a good time. Indeed, if you can combine your security needs with your dream realization needs, you will have strong goal-succeeding motivation. Address this need by answering this question: "What would I like to do if I did not have to work?"

List unmet dream-realization needs to be addressed:

_____   _____
_____   _____
_____   _____
_____   _____

UNDERSTANDING GOAL MANAGEMENT

How will you meet the needs you have listed? Through goal management. This book shows you how to use the key principles of goal management to meet your needs by defining, designing, and implementing goals. Remember these key principles:

1. Goals, like businesses, must be planned and managed.
2. Goals must be managed for both effectiveness and efficiency.
3. Time wasters and stressors defeat goals and must be eliminated.
4. Goals must be broken down into component parts.
5. Goals must meet personal needs and produce motivating rewards.
6. Goals are achieved through the performance of skills that have become habits.
7. You can't manage what you don't measure. As in TQM, target tasks must be measured, improved, and communicated.

Chapter 1 Checkpoints

✓ Understand the connection between needs, motivation, and goals.

✓ Define realistic and valuable goals.

✓ People—and even businesses—have five types of needs:
- Physical needs
- Security needs
- Caring-relationships needs
- Self-worth needs
- Dream-realization needs

2 | Time Wasters and Stress

This chapter will help you to:

- Prevent time wasters from defeating your goals.
- Use Worksheet 1 to solve on-the-job, personal, and home goal-management problems.

PROTECTING YOUR GOALS

How often have you failed to complete a task because a call or visitor interrupted you, or because you decided to switch to another task? How often have you given up on a goal because you seemed to be getting nowhere? These are time wasters that rob you of:

- **Time and resources.** They cause you to perform inefficiently, ineffectively, or both.
- **Energy and vitality.** Time wasters increase accidents and irritability and decrease sleep and exercise.
- **Your most cherished goals.** If not identified and checked, time wasters become addictive habits. Thus, most successful goal managers are also successful time managers.

Because time wasters rob us of time and goals, we call them *goal-time wasters*. This brings us to two important points: (1) Goal managers view time in relation to goals, which keeps their time focused on effectiveness, not just efficiency. (2) Time is not being wasted, goals are. Goals are always the most important concern, not time. Hence, all time should be "goal time." Every time you think of time wasters, you should ask, What goal is being wasted?

Goal-time wasters also create stress. *Stress* is the daily wear and tear on your body and mind that occurs every time your body responds to the people and situations in your life.

Whatever triggers stress is a stressor. The more intense the demand made on our body to readjust, the greater the stress, or wear and tear on our body. Though moderate, positive stress can motivate, energize, and focus you, negative, habitual stress can kill goals—and people. Chronic stress can cause many problems: headaches, neckaches, or backaches; muscular tension or pain; indigestion, ulcers, or an irritable digestive tract; fatigue or physical weakness; insomnia or sleeping difficulties; and depression. By causing such problems, stress itself becomes a major goal-time waster.

Stress can come from time-wasting habits such as starting a project at the last minute or not filing important papers carefully. Attitudes also create stress. Getting angry in a traffic jam when you can do nothing about it becomes a stressor that triggers your body's fight or flight response, which rapidly raises your blood pressure. The repeated stress of episodes like this creates problems. The same fight or flight response occurs when you dwell on the future and neglect important tasks in the present. Stress can also be caused by unhealthy habits: lack of exercise, excess weight, poor diet, inadequate sleep, and so on.

In short, goal-time waster and stressor habits are the invisible enemies of your goals. Successful goal management requires that you replace the destructive cycle that these habits create with a productive goal-management cycle.

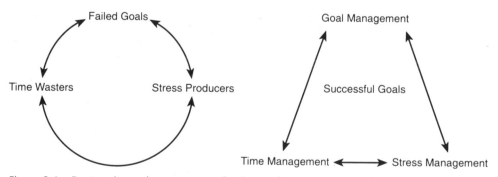

Figure 2.1   Destructive cycle versus a productive goal-management cycle.

This chapter will help you reach your goals by linking goal management to time and stress management.

THE GOAL-TIME WASTER INVENTORY

You have goal-time wasters in each of your environments—career, personal, and home. Goal-time wasters in all environments contribute to each other. Thus, your personal and home goal-time wasters contribute to your career goal-time wasters and vice versa.

What are your goal-time wasters? Pages 9-19 will help you identify them. Record how often each event creates problems for you on the "Frequency" line by using the following key:

0 = Never	3 = Once a week
1 = Once a month	4 = Once a day
2 = Twice a month	5 = Often each day

Write your rating in the space before the slash and use the space after the slash for a later review.

Career Goal-Time Wasters

C1—Interrupting visitors or phone calls. Do visitors or phone calls prevent you from completing project tasks?   Frequency _____/_____

Manage your interruptions or your interruptions will manage your work. Try being assertive, or ask coworkers to take messages for you. Try scheduling "block" times for phone calls, meetings, and quiet times.

C2—Not planning time, work, or goals. Do you find yourself working inefficiently because you do not plan out tasks in writing first?
Frequency _____/_____

C3—Unexpected crises. Do unexpected crises distract you from your planned tasks?   Frequency _____/_____

Tips ——————————————————————————————

Handling a Crisis

Prevention is the best strategy for crisis management. Try these ways to prevent a crisis:

1. Don't encourage "firefighter" coworkers, who create crises, then arrive to put out the fire, thus, becoming the indispensable office hero.

2. Reward good management, not just good rescue operations.

3. Look for and weed out any built-in crisis-producing procedures. (See C10.)

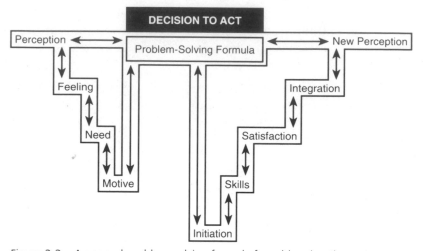

Figure 2.2   A general problem-solving formula for addressing time-wasters.

C4—Resisting goal and time management.   Are your efforts to manage your goals and time discouraged by coworkers or yourself?

Frequency _____/_____

Coworkers often sabotage time management because they think it calls for working harder. In reality, time management replaces *hard* work with *smart* work. Putting goal and time management reminders on your desk and wall, visibly carrying your goal management worksheets around the office, and practicing goal management tells others you're a serious goal manager. (See *Time Management* in the *Business Skills Express Series*.)

C5—Excessive socialization.   Does excessive socialization with coworkers reduce your efficiency?   Frequency _____/_____

Coworker requests have three parts: initial socialization, the request, and closing socialization. The request should take 90 percent of the time; each of the opening and closing segments should take no more than 5 percent of the time. So, if you talk to a coworker for 30 minutes, your hellos and good-byes and chitchat should take no more than 3 minutes. Otherwise, you're both procrastinating by socializing excessively.

C6—Disorganized self and/or coworkers.   Are poorly organized files a cause of your own or coworkers' inefficiency or ineffectiveness?

Frequency _____/_____

2

Personal disorganization is one of the first goal-time wasters to consider when you feel overwhelmed. A good rule: Never handle a piece of paper more than once or in a way that creates disorganization. If anyone needs more than 30 seconds to find something, you need more efficient systems of organization. (See P6 and H1.)

C7—Inefficient and/or ineffective meetings.   Do you feel that the meetings you attend are less than 70 percent efficient or effective?

Frequency _____/_____

C8—Inefficient or unclear communications.   Do poorly organized or incomplete communications get you behind in your work?

Frequency _____/_____

You can become a victim of inefficent communications in many ways: if a coworker interrupts you five times when all requests could be held for one call or meeting; if requests are not well organized or thought out; or if the requester has access to the information but is too lazy to "dig deeper." Inefficient and unclear communication can force you to delay critical decisions.

C9—Shifting directions and goals.   In midproject, do managers ask you to do it another way, cancel it, or start another project?

Frequency _____/_____

When you (or your managers) shift directions or goals in midstream, everyone is guilty of poor planning and will suffer its consequences. (See Chapter 5 on Planning.)

C10—Inefficient and/or ineffective procedures.   Do any built-in procedures in your department waste time and resources?

Frequency _____/_____

Procedures that are no longer efficient or effective create stress, bottlenecks, and wasted resources. Since most coworkers do not feel secure enough to "blow the whistle" on such procedures, use anonymous suggestion boxes or a time-management inventory.

C11—Confused authority or responsibility.   Do you lack the authority to make decisions about problems for which you are responsible?

Frequency _____/_____

2

Time is wasted when no one knows who "owns" the problem. When working in groups, be sure everyone knows who has final responsibility and authority.

C12—Undertrained coworkers. Are mistakes made or do jobs take too long because employees have not been properly trained?

Frequency _____/_____

C13—Not delegating. Do you get into binds that could have been avoided if you had asked someone to perform part of the task?

Frequency _____/_____

Do you try to do everything yourself? If so, you are playing superperson. (See P14.) Exchange tasks with friends or coworkers, each of you performing the tasks you are best at. Swap chores with home members. Do a coworker's filing in return for his or her proofreading of your reports. Study delegation techniques.

C14—Unclear career or organization vision. Does decision making or work become inefficient because either you or your organization do not have a clear vision to guide your decisions?   Frequency _____/_____

▮ Think About It

What are your top goal-time wasters at work? Review your responses to the career goal-time waster inventory. What are your three worst career goal-time wasters and in what situations do they occur? List at least one new routine you could use to eliminate each goal-time waster.

1. _____
   Situation _____
   New Routine _____

2. _____
   Situation _____
   New Routine _____

3. _____
   Situation _____
   New Routine _____

Personal Goal-Time Wasters

P1—Procrastination.   Do problems arise because you delay completing a task or leave tasks until the last minute?   Frequency _____/_____

You may put off tasks for many reasons: You choose a more pleasant task; you fail to break down the task into small parts that you can complete now and today; your subconscious tells you the task is really not a priority; you fear the consequences of reaching a goal, as your life may be permanently changed, and even positive change is stressful.

Tips ————————————————————————————

Ending Procrastination

You can overcome procrastination:

1. Discover and think through its causes.
2. Break down the avoided task into small, achievable 10- to 30-minute tasks and always at least start, promising yourself that you can quit whenever you like.
3. Plan your day and keep the plan.
4. Identify other goal-time wasters.
5. Surround yourself with visual reminders and motivators.
6. Describe the task in motivating terms.
7. Don't let perfectionism or the superperson syndrome legitimize delay. (See P14.)

P2—Information overload.   Do you try to solve too many problems at once or take in more information than you can handle?
                                      Frequency _____/_____

Scheduling too much into too little time or with too little energy creates information overload and a host of other goal-time wasters. In short, you're trying to solve too many problems at once, and probably none of them well. If you're only working on one problem but still experiencing information overload, then you've designed a poor solution to that problem.

P3—Not planning time, work, or goals. Do you often feel that you accomplish little during the day even though you are busy?

Frequency _____/_____

For every minute you plan your time, work, and goals, you will save three to four minutes. Planning has another important advantage: Despite all your daily distractions, it helps remind you of your goals, priorities, and targets—keeping you on course. (See Chapter 6.)

P4—Low self-discipline. How often do you say to yourself, "I'd rather watch TV than work on my goal task?"   Frequency _____/_____

You may lack self-discipline because you are tired, distracted, depressed, disinterested, not in the mood, or procrastinating. (See Chapter 4.)

Tips

Regaining Your Discipline

1. Schedule tasks in your appointment book at a time when interruptions are not likely to occur.
2. Stop competing activities such as TV.
3. Post very large and visible signs around your desk or home counters.
4. Boost your energy with a snack, brisk walk, or cup of coffee.

P5—Poor concentration. Do you have trouble concentrating on detailed tasks?   Frequency _____/_____

Review all goal-time wasters to locate the cause of your poor concentration. Focus on a small procedure or piece of the task. Once you have regained your concentration, don't think about your next task, as you will only create a new concentration block.

P6—Personal disorganization. Do you have to hunt for something because it is not where you thought it was?   Frequency _____/_____

Disorganization also affects your mood and motivation. Remember: You can't solve a problem unless you have achieved personal organization. (See C6 and H1.)

2

P7—Health problems.   Do you find that you change your plans or fall behind because of low energy or a health problem?

Frequency _____/_____

Low energy, chronic ailments, stress, poor diet, lack of exercise, poor monitoring of your health, or addiction to any substance or behavior can create health problems that waste time. Periodically review all goal-time wasters to see if any are contributing to the neglect of your health.

P8—Inefficient information-processing skills.   Do slow reading, poor memorization, and slow word processing delay your tasks?

Frequency _____/_____

P9—Not saying no to yourself or others.   Do you do tasks you shouldn't do or don't want to do because you find it hard to say no?

Frequency_____/_____

Most of us say yes to requests from others before we really think about the requests. The best response is "Maybe, let me check my calendar and get back to you." Protect your goals by protecting your time.

P10—Forgetting your life goals.   Do you feel that you are not getting where you want to be in life?   Frequency _____/_____

If you don't have a clear sense every day of your goals and a systematic plan to reach them, most likely you'll be busy without really getting ahead.

P11—Failure to follow up.   Do new problems develop because you forgot to follow up a task or postponed a decision?

Frequency _____/_____

Failure to follow up is the result of not considering the consequences of your action. Each time tasks are not followed up you risk creating new goal-time wasters.

P12—Resisting goal and time management.   Do you tell yourself, "I don't need to manage my goals and time better; I do well enough"?

Frequency_____/_____

You are the main cause of your resistance to goal-time management! You may have a lifetime of subtle but effective ways of diverting yourself from the tasks that you want to complete, and you may not have a strong system in place to ensure their completion. This book offers the tools you need to solve these problems. (See C4 and H5.)

P13—Anger and hostility.   How often do you find yourself getting angry at yourself or others?   Frequency _____/_____

Anger and hostility are stressors, and could lead to heart disease and high blood pressure. Try to replace anger and hostility with assertiveness and use stress-reduction techniques. (See P16.)

P14—Unrealistic expectations.   How often do you find yourself being a perfectionist or superperson?   Frequency _____/_____

Perfectionism—inappropriate and excessive thoroughness and neatness—is a habit that can destroy relationships, distract careers, and steal your time.

Superpersons are often perfectionists. Since superpersons try to do so many things, they often do nothing well. The causes could be unrealistic expectations and needs—financial, personal, career, emotional, materialistic. (Review Chapter 1.)

P15—Low self-esteem and low assertiveness.   Do you back off goals or situations because you feel unworthy and can't assert yourself?

Frequency _____/_____

Often low self-esteem and low assertiveness are simply the result of fear, which, once identified, can be eliminated through practice or therapy. Working on appropriate new skill goals will give you new confident habits.

P16—Lack of stress-reduction routines.   How often do you do things to reduce your stress?   Frequency _____/_____

■ **Tips**

Reducing Stress

Stress management can contribute greatly to goal-time management. To control stress, follow these guidelines:

1. As soon as stress appears in any part of your body, *slowly* breathe in and out at least three times, saying to yourself on your "out" breaths: "Let go of the tension in this area (or name the body part). It won't make a difference in my life in five years."

2. For at least 10 to 15 minutes a day, find a quiet, pleasant place and sit. Breathe deeply, relax your muscles, and think about nothing in particular for a minute or two. Then, think about your day and ask yourself what, if anything, has caused stress, and what you can do to avoid or reduce it. Write down and schedule ideas you want to implement.

3. For every 16 hours of work, set aside 1 hour to exercise, get a massage, meditate, or participate in some other kind of stress-reducing activity.

In any bookstore, you can find many books that describe other stress-reducing techniques.

■ **Think About It**

What are your top personal goal-time wasters? Review your responses to the personal goal-time waster inventory. What are your three worst personal goal-time wasters and in what situations do they occur? List at least one new routine you could use to eliminate each goal-time waster.

1. _____
   Situation _____
   New Routine _____

2. _____
   Situation _____
   New Routine _____

3. _____

     Situation _____

     New Routine _____

Home Goal-Time Wasters

Home goal-time wasters are similar to career and personal goal-time wasters. With approximately 90 household tasks needing to be performed regularly, the average household has the same need for professional management as a business. Indeed, the similarity between career and home goal-time wasters is often striking! Thus, you can use the same strategies to defeat home, career, and personal goal-time wasters.

H1—Disorganized spaces, records, and systems.   Do tasks at home fail to be completed due to poor organization and lack of systems?

                                        Frequency _____/_____

H2—No problem-solving or decision-making system.   Do members of your home fail to make joint decisions in an agreed manner?

                                        Frequency _____/_____

   Here's one solution to this goal-time waster: Have weekly home "staff" meetings and agree on a consistent problem-solving, decision-making system.

H3—Poor coordination.   Do home members fail to combine errands and share chores?   Frequency _____/_____

   Ask each household member to post day-by-day weekly to-do lists, including appointments, and place them side by side so you can trade tasks, combine errands, and be aware of each other's responsibilities.

H4—Neglect of problems.   Do problems arise because houshold tasks are neglected?   Frequency _____/_____

H5—Low goal-time management support.   Do home members fail to support each other's goal-management efforts?

                                        Frequency _____/_____

   Ask each member to evaluate your goal-time wasters.

H6—Unrealistic socialization.   Do the socialization habits and schedules of home members create problems?   Frequency _____/_____

H7—Low member involvement.   Do home members not get equally involved in the tasks and decisions of the home?

Frequency _____/_____

Regular weekly home staff meetings ensure involvement and mutual agreement. Remember this advice: If you want people to get involved in the problem, get them involved in the solution.

Think About It

What are your top home goal-time wasters? Review your responses to the home goal-time waster inventory. What are your two worst home goal-time wasters and in what situations do they occur? List at least one new routine you could use to eliminate each goal-time waster.

1. _____
   Situation _____
   New Routine _____
2. _____
   Situation _____
   New Routine _____

Interpreting Your Inventory Scores

Are you a goal-time waster or goal manager? To find out, add up the numbers you entered on each question in each inventory category.

Career goal-time waster score: First review___ /Second review___

Personal goal-time waster score: First review___ /Second review___

Home goal-time waster score: First review___ /Second review___

   Total inventory score   First review___ /Second review___

Now interpret your total inventory score:

Score Range	Interpretation
185–121	Your goals are being defeated by several goal-time wasters. Create goals to eliminate your many goal-time wasters.
120–91	Work on your goal-time wasters; they are holding you back.
90–61	You're a good goal manager, but have some areas needing improvement.
60 or less	You're an expert goal manager, but don't let overconfidence lower your guard.

Ideal Goal-Manager Scores for Each Section

Career: 22   Personal: 27   Home: 7   Ideal total score: 56

USING WORKSHEET 1: GOAL-TIME WASTERS

Because many of your goal-time wasters are habits, only constant attention will defeat them. Every week (monthly after you become a skilled goal manager) track your progress by reviewing Worksheet 1 on page 22. You can use Worksheet 1 in two key ways: (1) as a daily or weekly checklist, to identify frequent goal-time wasters; and (2) as an aid to problem solving, to analyze problems caused by goal-time wasters. For either use:

- First make a copy of the worksheet so that you will have a blank worksheet available for future use. (Please note: The copyright provision of this book allows you to make copies of worksheets for your use only.)

- When you consider a goal-time waster in one category, always review those in the other two categories. You learn the most about goal-time wasters if you realize how one influences the other.

- Ask coworkers and friends to evaluate the goal-time wasters you checked.

- Identify and challenge your goal-time wasters by talking about them to yourself and others.

■ Expanding What You Have Learned

What problems have you experienced at work during the last month? Select one to analyze. With this problem in mind, go through Worksheet 1 on page 22, checking all goal-time wasters that are contributing to the problem.

2

What goal-time waster is contributing most to the problem?

_____

What routine can you change to eliminate this goal-time waster?

_____

WORKSHEET 1: FINDING YOUR GOAL-TIME WASTERS

To Find Frequent Goal-Time Wasters

Analysis Period: From _____ to _____

During the week, tally each goal-time waster event to reveal your most frequent goal-time wasters.

For Problem Solving

State Problem:

Each time you experience *any* problem, review and check off all contributing goal-time wasters and see how they may be creating the difficulty.

Career Goal-Time Wasters

- [ ] C1 Interrupting visitors or phone calls
- [ ] C2 Not planning time, work, or goals
- [ ] C3 Unexpected crises
- [ ] C4 Resisting goal and time management
- [ ] C5 Excessive socialization
- [ ] C6 Disorganized self or coworkers
- [ ] C7 Inefficient or ineffective meetings
- [ ] C8 Inefficient/unclear communications
- [ ] C9 Shifting directions and goals
- [ ] C10 Inefficient or ineffective procedures
- [ ] C11 Confused authority/responsibility
- [ ] C12 Undertrained coworkers
- [ ] C13 Not delegating
- [ ] C14 Unclear career/organization vision

Personal Goal-Time Wasters

- [ ] P1 Procrastination
- [ ] P2 Information overload
- [ ] P3 Not planning time, work, or goals
- [ ] P4 Low self-discipline
- [ ] P5 Poor concentration
- [ ] P6 Personal disorganization
- [ ] P7 Health problems
- [ ] P8 Inefficient info-processing skills
- [ ] P9 Not saying no to self or others
- [ ] P10 Forgetting life goals
- [ ] P11 Failure to follow up
- [ ] P12 Resisting goal and time management
- [ ] P13 Anger and hostility
- [ ] P14 Unrealistic expectations
- [ ] P15 Low self-esteem/assertiveness
- [ ] P16 Lack of stress-reduction routines

Home Goal-Time Wasters

- [ ] H1 Disorganized spaces and records
- [ ] H2 No problem solving/decision making system
- [ ] H3 Poor coordination
- [ ] H4 Neglect of problems
- [ ] H5 Low goal–time management support
- [ ] H6 Unrealistic socialization
- [ ] H7 Low member involvement

Reminders:

Chapter 2 Checkpoints

✓ Protect your goals by eliminating your goal-time wasters. Practice, not just awareness, is needed to make these changes.

✓ Review Worksheet 1 weekly. Retake your goal-time waster inventory every three months and ask your friends and coworkers to assess your goal-time wasters using the same inventory questions.

✓ To solve *any* problem, first ask if it is caused by goal-time wasters.

3 | What Are Your Goals?

This chapter will help you to:

- Design goal tasks for all types of goals.
- Define rewards that motivate you to reach your goals.
- Create the three types of goals used in goal management to manage major goals:

  Image goals

  Skill goals

  Habit goals

TURNING A WISH INTO A GOAL

So far you have defined your needs and examined the many time wasters and stressors that block your way. Now you are ready to define your goals.

Goal Tasks: The Building Blocks of All Goals

Defining activities that, when completed, will result in a need being met is what goal definition is all about. The desire to meet a need without a commitment to perform a clear set of tasks is only a wish. The desire to meet a need by performing precise tasks is a goal. Systematic goal management provides the planning, persistence, and self-discipline you need.

All goals are reached by completing a series of tasks called **goal tasks** that move you toward your goal. Goal tasks perform the real work of the goal. Thus, goal management measures and evaluates goal tasks, not well-meaning statements and intentions. Defining goal tasks also brings a bonus. It helps you distinguish between important and unimportant activities. One way to avoid wasting time is to ask yourself constantly, "Is this a goal task—or a time waster or stressor?"

■ Putting It All Together

To see the relationship between needs and goal tasks, complete this exercise:

Assume You Want to Meet these Needs	Implied Goal	List Goal Tasks You Could Perform to Meet these Needs
Make more money (security)	Get a better job	Call network contacts Rehearse job interview Take time-management course
Complete these Examples		
Have more friends (self-esteem)	_____	_____ _____ _____
Lose weight (physical, self-esteem)	_____	_____ _____ _____

Reward Yourself!

Goal tasks have two parts: completion of the task and a reward. The reward will make you want to repeat the behavior. (This is also called positive reinforcement.)

Completed Task	Reward
Write two final pages of report	Next cup of coffee
No cigarettes in morning	Lunch with best friend
Call "lost" client with suggestion of work	10 minutes of *Sports Illustrated*

Finding rewards may be easier than you think. Ask your grandparents or parents what they considered rewards when they were younger and you might be surprised. Things that would have been regarded as rewards 40 years ago—going to a movie, dining at a restaurant, watching a popular TV program, reading a favorite out-of-town newspaper—are now considered ways of life that we are entitled to, no matter what we do. Only a few things such as expensive cars and vacations now seem like rewards. Because you can't give yourself a vacation after completing every goal task, you may think you have few rewards to motivate yourself. *But you can redefine events that you now take for granted as motivating rewards.*

Not all your creature comforts have to be transformed into rewards—just enough of them to serve as motivators. For example, keep the Saturday-night video rental as a family event, but make other video evenings rewards. Keep your morning rituals as nice things to do for yourself, but use the evening jog as a reward. Also, keep in mind that any positive consequence of your behavior can be rewarding. Thus, *avoiding negative consequences* is another possible reward for completing a goal task. If you don't have to admit to a coworker that you procrastinated again, for example, that is a reward. Here are some examples of possible positive rewards:

- **A new daily ritual:** An extra cup of coffee.
- **A new daily activity:** A daily gardening break; a 15-minute, stress-reducing shower.
- **Previously-planned future activities or purchases:** Next spring's wardrobe; next winter's vacation.
- **New possible, but realistic, future activities or purchases:** A fall weekend vacation; a new car.

To help you develop effective rewards for your goals and goal tasks, complete this exercise.

List your *present* daily rituals that could become effective rewards:	List *planned* future activities, routines, or purchases that could become rewards:
_____	_____
_____	_____
_____	_____
_____	_____
_____	

List daily *new* activities that could become effective rewards:	List *possible* future events, routines, or purchases that could become rewards:
_____	_____
_____	_____
_____	_____
_____	_____

3

Make Rewards Effective.   Follow these guidelines:

1. Link the reward clearly to the goal task and reward yourself only after (not before) the task is completed.

2. If you don't complete the task, don't give yourself the reward.

3. To qualify as a completed task, a task must have a measurable outcome, such as two final pages written, no cigarettes this morning, more than $300 in commissions earned today.

4. Select rewards that are fun, satisfying, stress reducing, varied, creative, and imaginative. These rewards provide maximum satisfaction and stress reduction.

Think About It

Can you see how rewards get wasted? Don Harding's boss is not happy with Don's monthly quality reports. Every morning Don blocks out an hour to work on reports. He starts out by chatting with his boss to get some direction. Then he gets a cup of coffee, flips through his favorite professional journals for ideas, bangs out a couple of very rough pages, and calls his wife to make plans for dinner. Every Friday, his stack of rough pages grows, but there is no monthly report.

1. How would you define his possible goal tasks? _____

_____

2. How would you define his rewards? _____

_____

3. How would you arrange his separate goal tasks and rewards? _____

_____

(See Feedback on Page 37.)

DEFINE "DOABLE" GOALS

Twelve months ago, Susan Wescott, MSW, quit her job as manager of a social services agency to begin a new career as a documentary film producer, a dream she has had since high school. Because she believes that producing a major work is her best way to break into the field, she spends most of her time looking for scripts and investors. She is hoping to produce an award-winning documentary on the struggles of women executives. So far she has spent $15,000 of her own money and has not been able to pay herself a salary. At the end of her first year, she still does not have a signed contract for her first production. After one year of 50-hour weeks she is very discouraged, but she is planning to stick with her strategy for another year. ■

Have you ever been where Susan Wescott is now? Keep her in mind as you think about defining your goals.

3

Let's start with this very basic principle of goal management: Just as business goals have subgoals, major personal goals are made up of three kinds of goals—image goals, skill goals, and habit goals.

Image Goals

Your dedication to a goal will grow if you visualize yourself accepting a reward for completing the goal. This visualization is your **image goal**—a primary personal goal that you visualize yourself reaching in one or two years. For example, you might see yourself walking into the boardroom to hear the announcement that you are being promoted because your monthly quality reports significantly improved company productivity. This image goal is a stronger motivator than the statement, "I want that promotion." Image goals are, thus, much more effective than *statement* goals.

Skill Goals

To perform the tasks required to complete an image goal, you need skills. For example, for Robert Williams to reach his image goal of seeing his book on the 1994 nonfiction *New York Times* Best-Seller List, he needs the skills of word processing, outlining, critical thinking, researching, editing, project management, and literary and editorial negotiation. Therefore, he needs to define and reach **skill goals** in order to reach his image goal.

■ **Think About It**

Is there a goal you have had for a long time but have not gotten around to working on? List all of the skills you will need in order to reach this goal:

Your image goal: _____

All needed skills: _____

3

Habit Goals

Skills do little good unless you use them regularly to reach an image goal. For example, you might have great proficiency in word processing, but if you do not use that skill regularly to improve your productivity how has the skill helped you? The skill must become a regular habit, such as daily writing. Skill goals develop the new skills needed to complete an image goal. **Habit goals** make sure the new skill is used regularly on goal tasks that complete the image goal. Chapters 5 and 6 will explain in detail the goal-management tools used for mastering new habits.

Figure 3.1   ACHIEVING YOUR GOALS: THE CYCLE OF SUCCESS

Needs

Clear Rewards and Consequences

Goal Tasks

Clear, Measurable Goals
Image Goals
Skills Goals
Habit Goals

WHAT ARE YOUR IMAGE GOALS?

Defining your image goals is like deciding where you want to go on vacation. If you make the wrong choice, you feel that you wasted your time and money.

You must spend time to decide the direction you want to take. (Don't procrastinate too long, however.) Worksheet 2 will help you define your image goals. (You will refer to this worksheet as you work through the book.) Take a moment now to complete the worksheet.

WORKSHEET 2: IDENTIFYING YOUR IMAGE GOALS

Directions:

1. Take two minutes to answer each question. You may use sentences to express your answers or "mind maps," like the one shown below.

2. Take another two minutes to revise your answers to each question.

3. Take another one minute per question to circle the best image goal. Also circle and label any statements that might represent skill or habit goals.

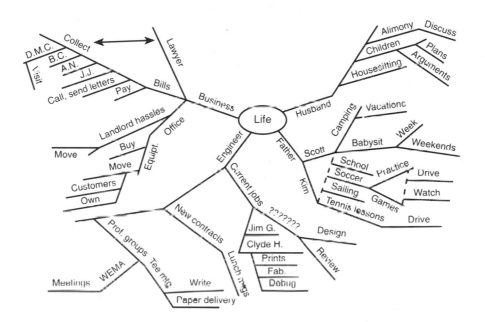

Question 1: During my life, I would like to achieve the following goals:

WORKSHEET 2: IDENTIFYING YOUR IMAGE GOALS (continued)

Question 2: I would like to spend the next three years doing the following:

Question 3: If I knew I was going to die in an accident six months from now, I would do the following until then:

Now that you have thought about them, you can define and commit yourself to your image goals. Each image goal has four components:

1. A well-conceived goal statement, such as "I want a promotion," "I want to quit smoking," "I want a successful marriage," or "I want to start my own business."
2. A precise reward for completing the image goal.
3. A precise and vivid image of the completed image goal and of its reward.
4. An image goal business plan, which includes many problem-solving components. The worksheets in this book make up your goal business plan.

Putting It All Together

Figure 3.1 "Achieving Your Goals: The Cycle of Success" on page 30 reviewed how goal concepts are tied together. Test your understanding by answering the following questions:

What are the four components of an image goal?

1. _____

2. _____

3. _____

4. _____

When do skill goals need to be defined?

_____

Why are habit goals so crucial to reaching your image goals?

_____

THE GOAL BUSINESS PLAN AND YOUR GOALS

Be sure your goals are ones you really want and need to pursue. Work-sheet 3 helps you decide. Look at the example Worksheet 3 on page 35. Now make a copy of the blank Worksheet 3 on page 36 and complete it. You will refer to Chapter 3 many times as you work through *Goal Management at Work*.

3

WORKSHEET 3: DEFINING YOUR GOALS

Statement of Goal	Image Goals	Skill Goals	Habit Goals
List each personal or career goal you would like to reach in the next year or two.	What images come to mind when you reach your goal, or just after? Select one.	What skills would you need in order to perform the goal tasks required to reach your goal?	What habits do you need in order to daily or regularly perform these goal tasks?
1. *Get promotion*	■ *Hearing my promotion announced at a board meeting* ■ *Boss calls me in to tell me* ■ *Coworkers' praise on hearing news*	■ *Organize and write a monthly quality report* ■ *Master statistics* ■ *Interview skills*	■ *Daily writing*
2. *Quit smoking*	■ *Accept award as one-year nonsmoker from company president, along with $1,000 bonus check* ■ *Home smells and looks great*	■ *Non-smoker skills* ■ *Handle "triggers"* ■ *Learn assertiveness*	■ *Daily exercise* ■ *Daily stress management* ■ *Coping strategies mastered*
3.			
4.			

Additional Possible Goals: *Lose weight, learn tennis*

WORKSHEET 3: DEFINING YOUR GOALS

Statement of Goal	Image Goals	Skill Goals	Habit Goals
List each personal or career goal you would like to reach in the next year or two.	What images come to mind when you reach your goal, or just after? Select one.	What skills would you need in order to perform the goal tasks required to reach your goal?	What habits do you need in order to daily or regularly perform these goal tasks?

1. _____

2. _____

3. _____

4. _____

Additional Possible Goals: _____

■ Expanding What You Have Learned

If Susan Westcott (review pages 28–29) had applied goal management to her new career goal, she would surely have had a better first year. How would you develop positive, success-oriented goal-management strategies for her second year?

1. What needs is Susan trying to meet through her new career? _____

_____

2. Does she have a realistic image goal? What would be the best image-goal statement for her? _____

_____

3. What skill goals does she need? _____

_____

4. What habit goals does she need? How could she turn her new skills into habits? _____

_____

5. What specific goal tasks could she define to measure her success and move towards her image goal? _____

_____

6. Do you think she uses rewards to motivate herself? _____

Feedback on Don Harding (page 28)

Check your responses to these:

1. Goal tasks: Outline entire report; review report draft weekly with boss; assemble company data; research; compare format with similar reports; rough draft; final draft.

2. Rewards: Chat with boss; coffee; professional journals; dinner with wife.

3. Arrangement of goal tasks and rewards: Rewards should come after each goal task is completed and at the end of the one-hour work session, including meeting with boss.

Chapter 3 Checkpoints

✓ Defining clear, motivating goals is the first secret to successful goal management. Without it, you can waste a lifetime pursuing the wrong goals.

✓ The desire to complete a goal must be strong enough to carry it to success.

✓ All major goals have three elements: image goals, skill goals, and habit goals.

✓ Routines, rituals, and things you take for granted can become effective rewards for completing daily goal tasks.

4 | Managing Goals Toward Success

This chapter will help you to:

- Use Worksheet 4, "Stages of a Goal Business Plan."
- Use Worksheet 5, "Managing Goals as Projects."
- Identify the goal–time-management skills you need.

IF YOU DON'T WANT TO MANAGE YOUR GOALS, YOU DON'T WANT THEM!

Managing a goal is like managing a business. If a business is not managed on a daily basis, it will surely fail. Daily management starts with a **business plan,** which includes time lines, revenue and output targets, marketing steps, and so on. To succeed in a business or with a goal, you have to start with a plan.

In Chapter 3, by defining your goals, you took the first step in developing business plans for your goals. In this chapter, we describe the next steps. But first, answer these questions:

	Image Goal 1	Image Goal 2	Image Goal 3
What are your image goals?	_____	_____	_____
What habit goals do you need to reach this image goal?	_____	_____	_____
What skill goals do you need to reach this habit goal?	_____	_____	_____

STARTING YOUR GOAL BUSINESS PLANS

How do you reach your defined goals? Figure 4.1, "Stages in Reaching a Goal," outlines a two-phase path:

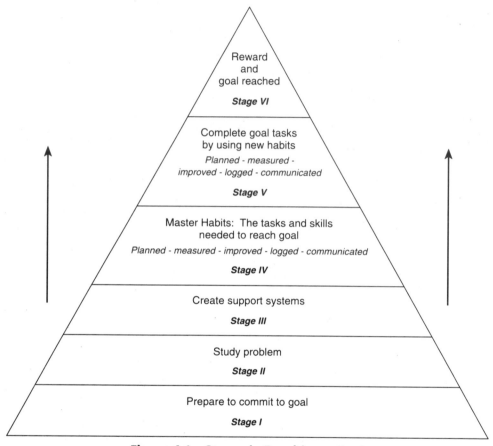

Figure 4.1   Stages in Reaching a Goal

Goal success depends on its early habit-formation stages. You cannot move closer to your goal without mastering the new habits on which each higher level depends. Goal tasks become easy if earlier stages are mastered. During all stages, especially through difficulties, keep recalling your image goal and its reward.

- Phase I: Short-term habit development. Master the skills and long-term habits to complete goal tasks. Complete Stages I, II, III, and IV of Figure 4.1.

- Phase II: Long-term completion of goal tasks. You perform goal tasks, organized as projects, over the long haul, resulting in the completed goal. Complete Stages V and VI of Figure 4.1.

To manage your goals, follow the stages outlined in Figure 4.1. Worksheet 4, "Stages of a Goal Business Plan," is a tool to help you. Based on Figure 4.1, review the sample worksheet, make a copy of the blank worksheet, and complete it as you read this chapter.

Using Worksheet 4

For each goal you listed in Worksheet 3, fill out a copy of Worksheet 4 on pages 44 and 45. (A sample is filled out on pages 42 and 43.) First, enter a clear, specific name for the goal. Use pencil, so you can make changes on future reviews. Check the box for each component under a stage *only* after you begin to implement your "action" entry for that component.

As you go through each stage, keep in mind that you can go back to earlier stages. If a problem comes up as you try to complete a component, go back to find the cause of the problem.

Stage I: Get Ready to Commit to the Goal

Readiness is important in all endeavors that require new behaviors, whether you are learning a sport, a mental skill, or a craft. Getting ready is setting yourself up for success.

Be ready to make a strong commitment to a well-thought-out goal that is realistic, doable, and highly motivating. Stages I, II, III, and IV of Worksheet 4 make sure you are ready to start your goal and that, when you do start, you succeed.

Stage II: Study the Goal Problem

Business plans for goals, like plans for new ventures, require research and creative problem solving. This stage has four components.

- *Research.* Make a thorough study of the goal, the need it will meet, and the possible ways to achieve the goal. Put pros, cons, thoughts, and options in writing.
- *Seek advice.* If you do not have all of the skills needed to research your goal, ask for help. Ask for advice, too, about your final ideas and plan, consulting experts if possible.

WORKSHEET 4: STAGES OF A GOAL BUSINESS PLAN

Directions: Use one worksheet for each image, skill, or habit goal. Using pencil, list your solutions. Check the box for each component only after you begin implementing it.

Goal from Worksheet 3: _____ *Daily Report Writing* _____

Stage I ◄————————————► Stage II ◄————————————► Stage III ◄————

Get Ready to Commit to Goal (Chapter 6)	**Study the Problem** (Chapters 3–6)	**Create Support Systems** (Chapter 3)
[X] Dissatisfactions that suggest goal *Want more challenge on job, and promotion*	[X] Research *Read "Manual of Style"*	[X] Use positive self-talk *Write new scripts*
[X] Needs that goal meets (see Chapter 1)	[X] Seek advice *Ask John*	[X] Create structure *14-day progress reports to boss*
Physical: *Use more $ for get-away vacations*	[X] Talk to friends and coworkers *Joan, Will*	[X] Redesign workspaces *Home study and office*
Security: *Better future on job*	[X] Evaluate alternative solutions and goal business plans *Do Project Management Worksheet*	[X] Create reminders and cues
Caring relationships:		[X] Organize for time and stress management *Redo file system*
Self-worth: *I need a more responsible job*		[X] Mentors *Who?*
Realizing dreams: *I want to be an author some day*		[X] Partners *Who?*
[X] Rewards to motivate commitment to goal *Wife and I will take cruise if get promotion*		[X] Coworkers *Joan and Will said yes*
[X] Define measurable, realistic goal *Monthly reports for 2 yrs gets me a promotion*		[ ] Friends
		[ ] Planners and logs *Start a 14-day writing habit log*

	→ Stage IV ←	→ Stage V ←	→ Stage VI

Master New Habit (Chapters 1–4)	**Complete Goal Tasks (Chapters 2, 4, 5)**	**Reach the Goal and Its Rewards (Chapter 8)**
☐ Develop habit needed to perform tasks of goal	☒ Plan goal tasks using Worksheet 5 on project management *Start this*	☐ Goal reached
☒ Define measurements for new habit *1 hour per day/1 page per day draft*	☐ Schedule goal tasks using Worksheet 9 *Start this*	☐ Receive your short- and long-term rewards
☐ Schedule and practice habits	☐ Measure, log, and improve goal tasks using Worksheet 10 *Start this*	
☐ Measure daily habit development		
☐ Improve techniques		
☐ Communicate to self and others		

4

WORKSHEET 4: STAGES OF A GOAL BUSINESS PLAN

Directions: Use one worksheet for each image, skill, or habit goal. Using pencil, list your solutions. Check the box for each component only after you begin implementing it.

Goal from Worksheet 3: _____

Stage I ⟵————⟶	Stage II ⟵————⟶	Stage III ⟵
Get Ready to Commit to Goal (Chapter 6)	**Study the Problem (Chapters 3–6)**	**Create Support Systems (Chapter 3)**

☐ Dissatisfactions that suggest goal

☐ Research

☐ Use positive self-talk

☐ Seek advice

☐ Needs that goal meets (see Chapter 1)

    Physical:

☐ Talk to friends and coworkers

☐ Create structure

    Security:

☐ Redesign workspaces

    Caring relationships:

☐ Evaluate alternative solutions and goal business plans

    Self-worth:

☐ Create reminders and cues

    Realizing dreams:

☐ Organize for time and stress management

☐ Mentors

☐ Rewards to motivate commitment to goal

☐ Partners

☐ Coworkers

☐ Define measurable, realistic goal

☐ Friends

☐ Planners and logs   Start a 14-day writing habit log.

WORKSHEET 4: STAGES OF A GOAL BUSINESS PLAN (continued)

→ **Stage IV** ←	→ **Stage V** ←	→ **Stage VI**
Master New Habit (Chapters 1–4)	**Complete Goal Tasks** (Chapters 2, 4, 5)	**Reach the Goal and Its Rewards** (Chapter 8)
☐ Develop habit needed to perform tasks of goal	☐ Plan goal tasks using Worksheet 5 on project management	☐ Goal reached
☐ Define measurements for new habit	☐ Schedule goal tasks using Worksheet 9	☐ Receive your short- and long-term rewards
☐ Schedule and practice habits	☐ Measure, log, and improve goal tasks using Worksheet 10	
☐ Measure daily habit development		
☐ Improve techniques		
☐ Communicate to self and others		

4

- *Talk to friends and coworkers.* Because they know your traits, your friends may be able to offer keen insight into whether your plans are likely to work for you. They can also offer invaluable support when a goal seems difficult and distant. But, if your friends are not support-ive, ask yourself, Do they really want the best for me?
- *Evaluate alternative solutions and goal business plans.* Before com-mitting to any goal business plan, generate several options. Test a plan for a week; then evaluate and redesign the plan, if necessary. Use Worksheet 5 on Page 51 for this component.

Stage III: Create Support Systems

Since your old habits will block your attempts to develop new ones, you need many support systems for your new habits. Your current habits have strong support systems that must be replaced and modified to support your new goals. These changes take time, but it is time well spent. Chapter 8 describes each component in this stage.

Stage IV: Master New Habits

Every time you remind yourself of an image goal, remind yourself of the habit it needs for success. Habit formation will probably be the most diffi-cult stage in attaining your goal. Since measuring your goal tasks is the only way to know if you are making real progress, keep daily records. Chapters 5 and 6 will help you schedule and practice habits, measure the daily development of your habit, improve your techniques, and communi-cate. Telling others, especially peers you respect, about your goals and deadlines is the best protection against procrastination.

Stage V: Complete Goal Tasks

As we discussed in Chapter 3, no matter what kind of goal you are pursu-ing, goal tasks must be completed to reach it. Chapters 5 and 6 include worksheets that will help you plan, measure, improve, and log your com-pleted tasks for each image, skill, and habit goal.

Stage VI: Reach the Goal and Its Rewards

If you set a clear, measurable goal, such as write three hours a day or quit smoking, you will know when you have reached your goal. This, of course, is the stage you have been seeking. For all of your goals, and goal tasks, be sure to give yourself the rewards you promised yourself.

MANAGING GOALS AS PROJECTS

Robert had a dream: to be an internationally known painter. His family and school counselors helped him identify the skills he needed to learn in high school and in college. With discipline and hard work, he mastered the skills and daily habits of a painter. By the end of college, he had won several awards and had, indeed, reached his skill and habit goals. But at 32 he gave up and took a job at his father's hardware store. At 45, as a seasoned manager of his dad's store, he reflected about how he had lost his dream: "I thought by simply painting well, the rest would take care of itself." ∎

What happened to Robert? His dream fell through a large gap between his goal tasks and his image goal—the planning gap. In managing goals, as in managing a business, you need to define, plan, and manage the many goal tasks required. And managing goal tasks as projects is the best way to plan these tasks and stick to your overall goal business plan. Indeed, projects are the largest components of your image goals. While Robert had appropriate skill and habit goals, his image goal was too vague—to be an internationally known painter—to focus his later work on a realistic, measurable goal. His weak image goal suggested no targets, such as "become an internationally known artist by winning the Chicago Art Institute Prize by 1989." Such a target would have focused his skills and habits. And organizing these skills and habits into a project would have provided him with a way to make sure his image goal tasks were paying off *and* a way to measure his progress. For instance, one of his early projects could have been to put on an exhibition in a local gallery, which would have been consistent with his image, skill, and habit goals.

Worksheet 5: Managing Goals as Projects

A goal business plan includes the definition and management of projects that are needed to reach a major image, skill, or habit goal. Worksheet 5, "Managing Goals as Projects," will serve your goals in these ways:

1. It tracks and measures results on the largest component of your goals, their projects.

2. It converts vague ideas into concrete plans for specific goal activities with schedules and marketing strategies. (You need marketing

strategies because, to reach most goals, you will need someone to help you or to purchase your time or product.)

3. It lets you know if your goals are realistic and doable and if you are procrastinating.

4. It works like a safety net under your goals. Many businesses fail and goals are not reached because important components are poorly executed, avoided, or omitted. Project outlines make sure you cover all your bases.

Using Worksheet 5

Review the sample Worksheet 5 and make a copy of the blank worksheet. Complete each section of the worksheet. For example, all image goals do have initial and potential clients or users of your new skills, habits, and final outcomes. Follow these guidelines for Worksheet 5:

1. Create at least one worksheet for each of your image, skill, and habit goals and one for each of the projects suggested by the goal tasks.

2. For large goal projects, you will need several worksheets, as you should break the project into subprojects, each having its own worksheet. For example, if you have an image-goal task to deliver a new Total Quality Management seminar in 1994, the project worksheet would include the following subprojects: (*a*) write a learner workbook, (*b*) write a trainer's manual, (*c*) develop marketing materials, (*d*) hire instructors, and (*e*) train instructors. Each subproject would have its own worksheet.

3. Be sure to review worksheets on your review dates. If you also give them quick reviews in the morning, you will stimulate your motivation and creativity.

4. Be convinced that this project management worksheet is important to the success of all of your goals:

Image, Skill, + Habit Goals ↔ Project Management ↔ Goal Tasks

Who would you hire to work on your team?

■ Expanding What You Have Learned

Think about the goals you listed at the beginning of the chapter and ask yourself:

What goal-time wasters do I need to reduce to reach this goal?	**What skills would I need to replace with a goal-time saver?**
Image Goal 1 _____	
_____	_____
_____	_____
_____	_____
Image Goal 2 _____	
_____	_____
_____	_____
_____	_____
Image Goal 3 _____	
_____	_____
_____	_____
_____	_____

Project: *Write monthly department reports*

Initial Clients: *Boss; company*

Project Partners: *Boss as mentor; John as editor*

Target Clients: *My boss; possibly future consulting clients*

Project Staff: *Boss as mentor; John as editor Gary & Barb as reviewers*

Project Deadline: *Complete 24 monthly reports by January 1996*

Mission: *Company wants better cost control; I want promotion & more job satisfaction*

Related Goals: *Get promotion at Board Meeting*

Review Dates:

☒ Image goal: *Meeting* .... *4/15* .... *5/15* *5/20*

☒ Skill goal: *Report writing, statistics*

☒ Habit goal: *Daily writing*

Measurable Performance Targets:

Target: *1 draft page per day* .... Deadline: *7/11/93*

Target: *Develop final report format and skills* .... Deadline: *9/5/93*

Target: *Complete statistics course* .... Deadline: *5/28/93*

Special Circumstances or Considerations:

See Page 2 for 1994 Target dates

Scheduled Start	Finish	Actual Start	Finish	Project Tasks (with Estimated Completion Time)
3/15	9/5	3/15		I. *Develop skills needed to write report*
3/15	4/15	3/19	4/10	A. *Read "Manual of Style"*
3/15	8/5	3/15		B. *Assemble and study internal & external sample reports*
6/21	8/15			C. *Take evening statistics course*
				D.
				E.
6/2	6/9			II. *Consult experts, friends, & ask for support/advice*
6/2	6/9			A. *Ask John to be editor or advisor; Gary or Barb as reviewers*
6/2	6/9			B. *Ask evening school professors before class starts*
				C.
				D.
				E.
5/1	1/7/95	5/1		III. *Develop daily writing habit*
5/1	1/7/95	5/1		A. *Write every 11 am–12 noon as "quiet hour;" have Jane take calls*
6/15	9/5			B. *Develop final report format*
				C.
				D.
				E.

Targeted Starting Dates for Above Project Tasks, Using Outline Numbers:

Month/Yr	Jan _95_	Feb _95_	Mar _94_	Apr _94_	May _94_	Jun _94_	Jul _94_	Aug _94_	Sep _94_	Oct _94_	Nov _94_	Dec _94_
First Week					III, A	II, A, B						
Second Week					III, B							
Third Week			I, A, B			I, C						
Fourth Week												
Fifth Week												

WORKSHEET 5: MANAGING GOALS AS PROJECTS

Page # _____ Project # _____

Project: [_____]

Initial Clients: _____

Project Partners: _____

Target Clients: _____

Project Staff: _____

_____

Project Deadline: _____

_____

Mission: _____

Related Goals:

☐ Image goal: _____

☐ Skill goal: _____

☐ Habit goal: _____

Review Dates:

_____ _____ _____ _____

_____ _____ _____ _____

_____ _____ _____ _____

Measurable Performance Targets:

Target: _____ Deadline: _____

Target: _____ Deadline: _____

Target: _____ Deadline: _____

Special Circumstances or Considerations:

Scheduled		Actual		Project Tasks (with Estimated Completion Time)
Start	Finish	Start	Finish	
				I.
				A.
				B.
				C.
				D.
				E.
				II.
				A.
				B.
				C.
				D.
				E.
				III.
				A.
				B.
				C.
				D.
				E.

Targeted Starting Dates for Above Project Tasks, Using Outline Numbers:

Month/Yr	Jan ___	Feb ___	Mar ___	Apr ___	May ___	Jun ___	Jul ___	Aug ___	Sep ___	Oct ___	Nov ___	Dec ___
First Week												
Second Week												
Third Week												
Fourth Week												
Fifth Week												

4

Chapter 4 Checkpoints

✓ Your goals, like a new business, must be managed. Create detailed plans and follow them daily.

✓ Are your goals realistic and feasible?

✓ Most image goals have companion skill goals and habit goals. Make sure these are all addressed.

✓ Organize your image goals, skill goals, and habit goals into projects and develop business plans to complete them.

5 | Planning Your Goals

This chapter will help you to:

- Practice the three crucial components of planning:

  1. Project and goal review.
  2. Daily scheduling and planning.
  3. Measuring and evaluating results.

- Use the goal business plan worksheets for three-year, one-year, weekly, and daily planning.

People don't plan to fail, they just fail to plan!

Anonymous

I know of no other way: To increase the likelihood of accomplishing important lifetime goals, you've got to plan your time each and every day.

Alan Lakein

Mr. Lee's $25,000 Tip

Not satisfied with his personal productivity, Charles Schwab, chairman of Bethlehem Steel Company in the 1930s, made this offer at lunch to one of his management consultants, Ivy Lee: "Show me how to get more done, and I'll pay you any reasonable fee." On the back of a menu, Lee wrote his now famous advice:

- *Every evening* write down the six most important tasks for tomorrow in order of importance.

- *Every morning* start working on Item 1 and stay on it until you're finished. Recheck your priorities and start on Item 2. If a task takes all day, don't worry, provided it's still your current Item 1.

  After any interruption, always return to that top priority task.

- *Now at the end of the day* tear up the list and start it over in the morning. If you didn't finish all of your items, don't worry, as you at least got your most important ones done. And without this system, you would not have even known what was most important.

- Make a habit of this every day.

- After it works for you, have your management team use it.

Asked how much he wanted for the advice, Lee told the chairman to send a check after using the system for several weeks. Schwab sent $25,000. After he and his management team implemented the advice for five years, Schwab claimed it resulted in Bethlehem Steel's emergence as the world's largest steel producer. Both he and his team were getting first things done first. Schwab claimed that the cost of the advice was the best investment Bethlehem had made all year. ■

IF YOU FAIL TO PLAN, YOU'RE PLANNING TO FAIL!

No other statement better summarizes the key to achieving your goals. As we pointed out in Chapter 4, goals—like businesses—need detailed, realistic, and measurable plans. However, having goal business plans is not enough. For these plans to succeed, they must be managed and measured *each day and at regular intervals*.

Think About It

Planning has brought you success. To show you how important planning is to your success, review your past successes and failures.

Your projects, goals, or enterprises that failed due to bad planning	Your projects, goals, or enterprises that succeeded due to good planning
_____	_____
_____	_____
_____	_____
_____	_____
_____	_____
_____	_____

Why Plan?

Time-management experts have found that:

1. Daily planning is the best and most powerful reminder of your goals.

2. Planning helps you discover if you are pursuing goals that are no longer important to you.

3. Planning protects your goals by focusing on what is important and what isn't.

4. Planning gives you control of time and stress now and in the future.

5. Planning proves that however busy you think you are, you have great flexibility in determining how you spend your time. You can change the commitments and goals that govern your present use of time.

6. Planning formalizes goals.

7. Planning *decreases* the time needed to carry out a project by at least 10 percent. *The more time you spend planning, the less time tasks take.*

8. Occasional planning does not work. Planning improves with practice.

The Basics of Goal-Management Planning

Managers often abandon planning after a few days because they don't give themselves enough time to get good at it. Planning takes practice and gets better each time you do it. You will find planning simple—and motivating—if you follow these basic steps, which, when completed, make up a goal business plan:

1. Complete Worksheets 4 and 5 for each major image goal, skill goal, or habit goal.

2. Complete the three-year and one-year multiple-project planners (Worksheets 6 and 7), which are described in the next section. *Use pencil*, which encourages originality and flexibility, for these and all worksheets.

3. Identify and memorize your goal-time wasters by using Worksheet 1 from Chapter 2.

4. Maintain a weekly goal manager (Worksheet 9).

5. Measure your goal task performance every day using Worksheet 10 in Chapter 6.

6. Spend 10 minutes at the beginning of each day reviewing your weekly goal manager, Worksheet 9, and Worksheets 3 through 5 for those goals you will be working on that day. Monday morning planning should be 20 minutes long, to also allow planning for the week.

LONG-TERM PLANNING

Most goals are long term. And most of the time, you will have several goals with many organized as projects. Long-term project planning then becomes the only way you can see how to set priorities and keep track of your goals' time and resources.

Worksheet 6 is a multiple-project planner for three years; Worksheet 7, for one year. Make a duplicate of each of them for future use. Before beginning a planner, review your completed versions of Worksheets 3 through 5. In fact, before beginning any planning process, *look over all previous goal business plan worksheets, especially Worksheets 3 and 4. These should be the only source of your goal tasks.*

As you complete these planners, notice how your motivation increases. This happens because plans help make the future more real and concrete. More importantly, they show where projects end, when goals are achieved, and show the rewards received.

DAILY PLANNING

Daily planning is the key to maintaining goal-achieving habits. It produces these benefits:

- Renewed and reenergized commitment to your goal each and every day.
- Identification of problems or mental blocks that may emerge, almost always unnoticed, to distract you from your new goal habits.
- Awareness of time expenditures that are resulting in effective and efficient action—or just keeping you busy.

WORKSHEET 6: THREE-YEAR PROJECT PLANNER

Directions: Use pencil. All entries should come from Worksheet 5. For each quarter, state the major milestone and enter specific project goal tasks.

Projects:

1. _____   4. _____
2. _____   5. _____
3. _____

Special circumstances or principles:

Winter 199___	Spring 199___	Summer 199___
Milestone:		
Proj. 1		
Proj. 2		
Proj. 3		
Proj. 4		
Proj. 5		

Fall 199___	Winter 199___	Spring 199___
Milestone:		
Proj. 1		
Proj. 2		
Proj. 3		
Proj. 4		
Proj. 5		

Summer 199___	Fall 199___	Winter 199___
Milestone:		
Proj. 1		
Proj. 2		
Proj. 3		
Proj. 4		
Proj. 5		

Spring 199___	Summer 199___	Fall 199___
Milestone:		
Proj. 1		
Proj. 2		
Proj. 3		
Proj. 4		
Proj. 5		

WORKSHEET 7: ONE-YEAR PROJECT PLANNER

Directions: Use pencil. All entries should come from Worksheets 5 and 6. For each month, state the major milestone and enter specific project goal tasks.

Projects:

1. _____   4. _____
2. _____   5. _____
3. _____

Special circumstances or principles: _____

January	February	March
Milestone:		
Proj. 1		
Proj. 2		
Proj. 3		
Proj. 4		
Proj. 5		

April	May	June
Milestone:		
Proj. 1		
Proj. 2		
Proj. 3		
Proj. 4		
Proj. 5		

July	August	September
Milestone:		
Proj. 1		
Proj. 2		
Proj. 3		
Proj. 4		
Proj. 5		

October	November	December
Milestone:		
Proj. 1		
Proj. 2		
Proj. 3		
Proj. 4		
Proj. 5		

Daily Time and Stress Diagnostic Log

Virtually every time-management expert insists that, before beginning development of time-management skills, managers complete an analysis of how they spend and misspend their time. Worksheet 8 provides a vehicle for recording and analyzing how you use your time each day.

You can use Worksheet 8 in three ways:

1. As a record of how you spend your time.
2. As a record of your goal-time wasters. If you use Worksheet 8 together with the goal-time waster checklist in Worksheet 1, you will soon be able to identify and head off goal-time wasters before they occur.
3. As a daily planner and log, allowing you to compare what you intended with what you did.

■ **Think About It**

At the end of each day, after completing Worksheet 8, ask yourself these questions:

1. On which image, skill, or habit goals did you make measurable progress today?
2. Did you get right into your most important task for the day, or did you put it off?
3. Is this how you wanted to spend your time? If not, what could you have done differently? Are your tasks poorly designed or managed, or are you pursuing the wrong goals?
4. What is the impact of interruptions on your productivity?
   - Did you act constructively to limit interruptions and manage them when they did occur?
   - What are your most common interruptions?
   - How many interruptions could you have avoided with better planning or assertiveness?
   - How many interrupted tasks did you leave unfinished at the end of each day?
5. What tasks should you not have done at all?

WORKSHEET 8: WHERE DOES YOUR TIME GO?

Day _____ Date _____

Directions: Make a check mark in Actual Task Performed column if you perform scheduled task. If scheduled task is not performed, enter actual task. Tally and ask appropriate questions about your total time usage at bottom of worksheet.

Day's Top Priority Tasks

1. _____
2. _____
3. _____
4. Plan/Organize/Solve _____

5. Meetings _____
6. Routines _____
7. Interruptions _____
8. Urgent _____

	Scheduled Task	Sch'd Task Number	Actual Task Performed	Actual Task Number	Goal-Time Waster Number	Goal-Time Saver Used (+) or Suggested (*)
6						
7						
8						
9						
10						
11						
12						
1						
2						
3						
4						
5						
6						
7						
8						
9						

Total Hours and Minutes Spent on Activities:

1st Priority Task ____	Planning/Org. ____	Interruptions ____	Reading ____
2nd Priority Task ____	Meetings ____	Urgent/Crises ____	TV ____
3rd Priority Task ____	Routines ____	Other ____	Sleep/Rest ____

5

6. Which tasks could've been done later when they wouldn't have interfered with an important goal task?

7. Could you have delegated more tasks?

8. What tasks could you have:
   - Simplifed, such as answering correspondence by noting actions on the requesting correspondence?
   - Done faster, like skimming journals, dictating while in the car, and so on?

9. With which coworkers do you spend the most time? How long? How often? Are these contacts the best for reaching your goals?

10. Which goal-time wasters keep popping up and need to be eliminated?

Know Your Energy Levels

Good daily planning starts with matching your goal tasks and daily routines with your energy levels. Ask: *"Am I a morning or an evening person?"* You know that you get your best work done at one time or another. Not only are you either a morning or night person, but you have energy cycles throughout the day. Whatever type you are, your efficiency *all day* will increase strikingly if you arrange your tasks as much as possible around your daily energy cycles.

Energy Insights

A manager, who is now a CEO, was unable to make his morning staff meetings completely productive even though he was disciplined enough to hold them every morning at 9 AM. One night he watched a documentary on biorhythms and concluded that he ought to reschedule his meetings during one of his "high-energy" hours, which he realized were from 11 AM to 3 PM.

By the fourth day of his new 11–12 noon daily staff meetings, he noticed a difference: He felt more in control, was able to more quickly grasp the problems, suggest solutions, and chart a critical path; he also realized that his note-taking and listening skills improved. By the end of the second week of this new schedule, his staff actually looked forward to the meetings, because he had become a better facilitator. Within two years, he knew he would become CEO. ∎

To take advantage of his new insight, the manager mapped his energy levels and began to schedule his other work routines around these levels:

His Energy Level	What Is Your Energy Level at These Times?
7 AM–10 AM: Low Energy	_____
11 AM–3 PM: High Energy	_____
3 PM–6 PM: Moderate Energy	_____
7 PM–9 PM: Low Energy	_____
9 PM–11 PM: Moderate Energy	_____

MATCHING YOUR TASKS TO YOUR ENERGY LEVELS

Energy Level	Task Mismatches	Good Task Matches	Your Best Task Match (List Your Specific Tasks)
High energy	Opening mail	Top priority tasks	_____
	Reading newspaper	High concentration tasks	_____
	Unneeded coffee break	Unpleasant/stressful tasks	_____
		Original-thinking tasks	_____
		Disliked routine tasks	_____
		Procrastinated tasks	_____
		Major reorganizing tasks	_____
		Chairing meetings	_____
Moderate energy	High- or low-energy tasks	Attending meetings	_____
		Ordinary correspondence	_____
		Returning/making phone calls	_____
Low energy	High-energy tasks	Sign letters	_____
		Plan the next day	_____
		Professional/personal reading	_____
		Brief, needed coworker chat	_____
		Snack, coffee break	_____
		Stress-management exercises	_____

THE WEEKLY GOAL MANAGER

So far, you have planned projects over three years and over one year and have analyzed how you spend your time each day. One additional step is to complete a goal business plan on a daily basis: the weekly goal manager, such a powerful goal-management tool that many use it as their daily appointment calendar.

While most goal business plan worksheets are used for reference and long-term planning, you will use the weekly goal managers, along with Worksheets 1 and 5, *every day*.

Worksheet 9, the "Weekly Goal Manager," should take no more than five minutes per day to complete. Make copies of the blank worksheet. Before completing it, review the sample "Weekly Goal Manager." Notice these useful features:

Goal Tasks Achievable This Week.   Select these by reviewing Worksheet 5 and choosing three goal tasks that you can complete this week.

Schedule Column.   Remember that scheduling should take your energy levels into account. List blocks of time for a typical day. For example, one block of time might be for creative tasks, return calls, report writing, or week's priority goal tasks.

Weekdays.   Each day, in half-hour segments, plan the day's goal tasks, specific tasks during your block times, and scheduled commitments and appointments. Give yourself half-hour transitions to allow for the interruptions and overtime.

Check Mark/Interruption Column.   Check each goal task as it is completed. If a task is not completed, turn the page sideways and describe why. Highlight in yellow the interrupted or uncompleted tasks. It should be continued the *same day* if possible until completed. If not completed, reschedule it during the week.

Daily and Weekly Target Monitor.   In the top row, create headings that represent your most common daily goal tasks and frequent activities. Enter daily and weekly targets for the amount of time each should take. Each day, enter the time you spend on that task or activity. At the end of the week, total all columns so you can compare them with your targets. By using this monitor, you will be adopting the habit of daily tracking.

WORKSHEET 9: WEEKLY GOAL MANAGER

Week of _March 8_

Image goals/Rewards 1. _Get Promotion at Board Meeting/Fun Winter Vacation_ 2. _Smoke-Free Home! New Car_ 3. _____

Skill or habit goals _1-Hour Daily Writing on Reports_ _Learn nonsmoker skills_ _____

Date started: _1/15_   Date started: _3/1_   Date started: _____

Goal Tasks and To-Do Tasks Achievable This Week!

1. _Outline of March Dept. Report_
2. _List Statistics Course options_
3. _____
4. Plan/Organize/Solve _Org. Files_

5. Procrastination tasks _John's performance review_
6. Errand/Routine/Urgent _Gift for Joan_
7. Exercise _Jog every other morning_
8. Self-care & support _Call Dad_

Attach Worksheet 1

	Mon 8	Tue 9	Wed 10	Thu 11	Fri 12	Sat 13	Sun 14
Day's Diary:		✓ Report	✓ Promotion	✓ Annual mtg	✓		NFL
Problem-Solving Runs	Run	✓	Run			Run	Run
7 News/Organize		✓				Tennis	
Breakfast/Chores		✓					
8 Committee		✓					
Creative Tasks	Plan	✓ Plan	Plan ✓	Plan	Plan	✓	
9	Report	✓ Report	✓ Report	✓ Report	John called	Report	✓
	Outline	✓ Outline	✓ Outline	✓ Outline		Outline	
10	Dictation	✓					
	Calls	✓					
11 Staff Meeting	Staff	✓ Staff	✓ Staff	Staff	✓ Staff	✓	Church
	Meeting	✓ Meeting	✓ Meeting	✓ Meeting	Meeting	✓	Church
12							↓
Lunch/Brisk Walk			Lunch	✓			
1		Revise	with Boss ✓	✓			Dinner
		Report ✓	↓	✓			at
2		↓					Mom's
3	Staffing ✓						↓
	Analysis ✓			Call Will ✓			↓
4				John, called ✓			
5							
6							
News/Chores							
7 Dinner/Family							
8 Personal Goal Tasks	Smoke Enders ✓					✓	
↓	"Triggers" ✓						
Day's Goal-Time Wasters:		P4	Mom called	C7,	C1, C2,		

Daily and Weekly Target Monitor

Tasks	Diet	Plan/Org.	Exercise	Stress Mg.	Self Care	Support	Career	J-G Tasks	Work	Read	Total	Errands	Sleep	Misc.	R/TV
Targets (Day/Wk)	3 Coffee/21	.5/3	.5/3	.5/3	1/7	1/5	.25/2	2/12	8/40	1/5	14.75/90	2/14	8.0/56	—	1.5/10
M	6	.5	.5	0	1.0	1.0	.5	2.0	8.0	.5	14.0	1.0	8.0	1.0	0
T	4	2.0	0	.25	1.0	.5	.25	1.0	8.0	0	13.5	2.0	7.0	1.0	.5
W	4	.5	.5	.25	1.0	.5	0	2.0	8.0	0	12.75	2.0	8.0	1.25	0
Th	3	0	0	0	1.0	1.0	0	1.5	9.5	0	13.0	1.5	8.0	1.5	0
F	3	.25	.5	0	1.0	0	0	2.0	8.0	1.0	12.75	1.0	7.0	3.25	0
Sat	3	.25	0	.5	1.0	1.0	.5	1.0	0	1.5	5.75	2.0	8.0	7.25	1.0
Sun	3	0	.5	0	1.0	.5	0	1.0	2.0	0	5.0	2.0	8.0	7.0	2.0
Total		3.5	2.0	1.0	7.0	4.5	1.25	10.5	43.5	3.0	76.0	11.5	54.0		3.5

WORKSHEET 9: WEEKLY GOAL MANAGER

Week of

Image goals/Rewards   1. _____   2. _____   3. _____

Skill or habit goals   _____   _____   _____

Date started: _____   Date started: _____   Date started: _____

Goal Tasks and To-Do Tasks Achievable This Week!

1. _____   5. Procrastination tasks _____

2. _____   6. Errand/Routine/Urgent _____

3. _____   7. Exercise _____

4. Plan/Organize/Solve _____   8. Self-care & support _____

Attach Worksheet 1

	Mon___	Tue___	Wed___	Thu___	Fri___	Sat___ Sun___
Day's Diary:		√	√	√	√	√
7						
8						
9						
10						
11						
12						
1						
2						
3						
4						
5						
6						
7						
8						
Day's Goal-Time Wasters						

Daily and Weekly Target Monitor

Tasks Targets (Day/Wk)											
M											
T											
W											
Th											
F											
Sat											
Sun											
Total											

Make Notes at Bottom.   As new insights about your goal-management or work experiences occur to you, note them at the bottom for possible use in your next "Weekly Goal Manager."

Tips ————————————————————————

Using the Weekly Goal Manager

- Plan each day and each week—no excuse!
- Always use a pencil to fill out the worksheet.
- Take your weekly goal manager everywhere. Clip it to your desk appointment book, or fold it as an insert in a pocket-size appointment book. If it's in your way, you'll have to handle it—and use it.
- At the end of each week, look over the weekly goal manager to see what went right and what went wrong. Your next weekly goal manager should take this into account.
- On the first day you use a new weekly goal manager, check all the goal-time wasters that you need to work on. They might suggest new skill goals.

Expanding What You Have Learned

Broaden your understanding about goal-management planning by considering the following questions:

How do you think daily planning will improve your daily performance on:

Your daily routines?_____

Your goals?_____

You may resist planning because it is *thinking* rather than *doing*. Can you anticipate the problems you might have with daily planning—and the solutions? On page 67, jot down potential problems and possible solutions.

Problems	Solutions

You can increase your energy level during the work day with 20 minutes of aerobic exercise, like brisk walking or jogging. When would you get the most benefit from such exercise?

5

Chapter 5 Checkpoints

Not only is daily goal-management planning motivating, but it is essential to success!

✓ Take your planning worksheets everywhere.

✓ Once you start daily planning, you will see these changes:

- You will be more eager to start the day.

- You will set more deadlines—and meet them without stress.

- You will become more aware of your goal-time wasters and your progress in eliminating them.

✓ You'll get better at planning as time goes on—don't worry!

6 | Measuring New Habits

This chapter will help you to:

- Develop the habits needed to master your career and personal goals.
- Apply the three basic steps of Total Quality Management: Measure, Improve, and Communicate to Self and Others.
- Create a habit-goal log.

HABITS OF SUCCESS

For many of us, the word *habit* calls up sacrifice and drudgery, being compulsive and uncreative. But think of the people like yourself who succeeded because they developed **habits of success** through daily study and practice—often against adversity—until they reached their goals:

- Peter Werner is a CEO. After joining his company at age 22, he studied for five years every night after his kids went to bed and got his MBA. During his 30s, he spent every Friday inspecting plant sites. By age 41, he was the CEO.

- Hillary Rodham had a goal statement she formulated in high school: "Make a difference in politics." She knew she needed the skills to think on her feet, so she joined the debating team and student government—despite the resistance to girls as leaders. She also mastered the skills and habits of academic study, enabling her to complete a law degree. She single-mindedly focused on her law and political career. Hillary eventually became First Lady. Her high school friends, however, know she hasn't reached one of the image goals we all knew she had: Being sworn in on Inauguration Day as president of the United States.

- John Swiderski never had time during college to be on the squash team. Starting at age 35, he joined a Saturday morning round-robin tournament league. He missed only three mornings for vacations. He won his first tournament after a year. ■

This chapter gives you tools to help you form—like Peter, Hillary, and John—your own habits of success.

TOTAL QUALITY MANAGEMENT

Leaving your career and goals to luck or relying on such mottos as "fake it 'til you make it," "hit or miss," and "wait it out and hope for the best" is easy—but dangerous. These shortcuts leave you without the habits needed to reach future goals.

As we have said several times, *"To reach your goals you must manage them, and managing goals is like managing a business."* You can never repeat this motto too often to yourself—and you never have to fear its outcome.

What does this mean in practice? In managing your goals, you can follow the lead of many successful managers who are applying **Total Quality Management (TQM).** Its underlying principle is: Constant measurement is the only way to determine if performance standards are being maintained and improved. Put another way, "You can't expect what you don't inspect!" This principle of TQM tells you to do three things constantly: (1) measure, (2) improve, and (3) communicate the results to yourself and everyone involved.

GETTING STARTED

Even after you realize that a new habit is the key to reaching an important goal, you might focus on the habits you lack. Instead, remind yourself why you are more likely to succeed than to fail. Start by reviewing past successes that you will draw on to complete your new goals.

■ **T h i n k   A b o u t   I t**

Your life is full of successes! List your successes, starting as early as you can remember them as a child:

Developing new skills:

_____

_____

_____

Starting new ventures, organizations, or projects:

_____

_____

_____

Implementing new ideas:

_____

_____

_____

Career or personal successes achieved because of a habit:	Habit that made it possible:
_____	_____
_____	_____
_____	_____

If you ever doubt that you can make it to the finish line with your new goals and supporting habits, review these lists. You *will* succeed if you rely on habits, not self-defeating shortcuts.

Identifying Needed Habits

New habits are hard to learn for one simple reason: Old habits pull you strongly in the opposite direction. Thus, you must both extinguish old, interfering habits and develop new ones.

6

To get ready to form your *habits of success*, first identify the goals you want to track and old habits that might get in your way.

List at least three goals (image goals, skill goals, or habit goals) that you want to master during the next 28 days:

1. _____

2. _____

3. _____

What goal-time wasting habits could defeat your habit-formation efforts in the next 28 days? (See Chapter 2.)

_____   _____

_____   _____

_____   _____

Start Small

Don't set yourself up for failure. Keep this motto in mind: *Start small, start simply, and gradually set higher standards.* If your image goal is "Because of the 12-page monthly quality reports I handed to my boss, I get my promotion at the annual board meeting" and your habit goal is "daily writing," you might start with the target goal task of writing 15 minutes every day. That is enough to get you into the habit of writing, researching, and scheduling the task.

28 DAYS TO A HABIT OF SUCCESS

The process of creating good, new habits takes about 28 days. If you complete two of the 14-day habit logs presented here as Worksheet 10, you will create your first new habit of success.

Logs help you practice this management principle: You can't manage what you don't measure. A log, thus, puts you in control, keeps you on track, and gives you a better chance of moving forward with satisfaction and accomplishment.

1 WORKSHEET 10: GOAL-HABIT LOG # _____

2
Skill Goal ___Learn how to organize a Dept. report___
Image Goal ___Hand 12-Page Monthly Report to Boss___

3 Needed Habit Goal ___Daily Writing___

5 Image-Goal Reward ___1995 Winter Mexico Vacation___

4 14-Day Goal Task ___Finish 1st Draft___
14-Day Reward ___Go to movies with Jean___

6 Month M/D Date	**7** Min. Time Target 15-min. per day	**8** Target 1 Measure 1 Page Rough notes	**9** Target 2 Measure 1 Final Draft Page	**10** Target 3 Measure Reviewed with Jean	**11** Goal-Time Wasters Blocking New Habit	**12** Solutions to Blocks	**13** Insights and Self-Talk
21	✓	1			Phone Interruptions	Have Receptionist take	"I'm out of my league."
22	30	2	1	✓		messages	Replace with
23	✓	1					"When I get this mastered,
24	✓		1				I'll get that promotion!"
25					Boss dropped in	Should have simply	
26	45	2	1	✓		started after he left	
27	✓	1					
28	✓						
29	✓						
30	30	2	2	✓	Staff meeting went over,	Use meeting agendas	
1	✓				but stayed with it		
2	45	3	3		Got stuck on numbers	Ask John at college to help	Take a statistic course
3	30	2	2				Had great session.*
4	30	2	2	✓			
14 Totals:	13 days	12 pages	12 pages	4 Reviews			

New Insights To Memorize: 15 ___Visualize your great March 13 session & repeat it.___

6

1 WORKSHEET 10: GOAL-HABIT LOG # _____

2
Skill Goal _____
Image Goal _____

3
Needed
Habit Goal _____

5
Image-Goal
Reward _____

4
14-Day
Goal Task _____

14-Day
Reward _____

6 Month	**7** Min. Time Target	**8** Target 1 Measure	**9** Target 2 Measure	**10** Target 3 Measure	**11** Goal-Time Wasters Blocking New Habit	**12** Solutions to Blocks	**13** Insights and Self-Talk
Date							
_____	_____	_____	_____	_____	_____	_____	_____
_____	_____	_____	_____	_____	_____	_____	_____
_____	_____	_____	_____	_____	_____	_____	_____
_____	_____	_____	_____	_____	_____	_____	_____
_____	_____	_____	_____	_____	_____	_____	_____
_____	_____	_____	_____	_____	_____	_____	_____
_____	_____	_____	_____	_____	_____	_____	_____
_____	_____	_____	_____	_____	_____	_____	_____
_____	_____	_____	_____	_____	_____	_____	_____
_____	_____	_____	_____	_____	_____	_____	_____

14
Totals: _____

New Insights
To Memorize: **15**

The Goal-Habit Log

A sample Worksheet 10, "Goal-Habit Log," with numbered sections and examples, is included for the image goal: "Because of the 12-page monthly quality reports I handed to my boss, I get my promotion at the annual board meeting." There is also a blank copy of Worksheet 10, which you should copy for future use. Fill in Worksheet 10 as you go through the following review of this log.

Each day, measure and record target tasks in the log. The table below explains each section of the log.

Log Section	How to Complete Your Log
Section 1 Title and Log #____	Prepare one log for each goal and number each log. Staple logs together, behind your weekly goal manager, Worksheet 9.
Section 2 Skill goal or image goal	Use the Chapter 3 and 4 worksheets to select your goals. You can have many skill-goal logs for one image goal, as you may need many new skills.
Section 3 Needed habit goal	Record the habit goal for this log in simple terms that tell you what behavior you will engage in each day.
Section 4 14-day goal task(s)	List clear, specific activities needed to practice the desired habit.
Section 5 Rewards	List the reward you will give yourself *if and only if you* complete your targets. Make rewards realistic and motivating.
Section 6 Month and date	Date your log by noting the capital letter of the month(s), with dates below.
Section 7 Minimum time target	Enter the minimal time you want to spend developing your habit, usually stated in "per day" terms. Start out with the shortest possible practice period, usually 15 minutes. Increase this period gradually as appropriate.

6

Section 8
Target 1 measure

Select targets that are the outputs that you want and can be measured, such as two final pages rather than work 2 hours.

Section 9
Target 2 measure

See Section 8. You need more than one meaningful target with which to measure your progress.

Section 10
Target 3 measure (Optional)

See Section 8. You may not need a Target 3.

Section 11
Goal-time wasters blocking new habit

Identify the goal-time waster habits blocking your progress and enter them. If they keep emerging, spend a week or two working on a new goal-time saving skill goal, resulting in new goal-supporting habits.

Section 12
Solutions to blocks

Note here solutions to your goal-time wasters.

Section 13
Insights and positive or negative self-talk

Enter and review daily any insights that come to mind as you practice your skill or habit. Apply them appropriately. Record any negative self-talk that recurs as you practice, replacing it with new positive self-talk. (See Chapter 8.)

Section 14
Totals

Though you will note your progress daily, after 14 days you will want to calculate your totals and divide them by 14 to get your daily averages. Ask: "Would other targets better measure my progress?"

Section 15
New insights to memorize

Circle insights from Sections 11 to 13 and enter them here. Enter them in your next log and memorize them.

As you practice your goal habit and logging, you will find great satisfaction in sitting down to log in each entry—like seeing your new, higher bank balance every time you deposit money.

After about a week, you will ask, "Which of the time slots would I like to fill in next or increase?" It becomes a game. You find yourself performing a habit task for two reasons: You want or need to do it, or you want the satisfaction of recording your progress. Either way, the habit becomes ingrained.

Tips

Successful Habit Logging

1. Clip all logs together behind your weekly goal manager (Worksheet 9). Set them down where they will stand out—by the phone, by your computer.

2. Schedule habit-formation sessions during the same period—block time—each day.

3. If you fall behind for a day or two because of travel or deadlines, simply schedule a catch-up day and don't worry about the lapse. Get back on track and don't abandon your habit goal or regimen.

4. Even though you may have realized in Chapter 5 that you are an evening person, if you have problems sticking to a habit-formation schedule, you might want to start out in the morning, when there are the fewest interruptions. Studies consistently show that managers who exercise in the morning stick to it more than those who exercise in the afternoon or evening. The same is true of most daily habits.

6

Creating Habit Clusters

If you create clusters of tasks that are performed in one period of activity, each task will become easier, especially your goal-habit tasks.

Clusters should usually last about an hour. They often have a 30-minute anchor task, like those shown in bold in the following examples of habit clusters. Create your own below the examples and test them:

Exercise, Shower/dress, breakfast and **time-management planning**
Your cluster: _____

Get coffee, review day's work with staff, hold calls, **30-minute writing**
Your cluster: _____

Dictation, **2 draft pages of dept. report**, lunchtime walk instead of smoking
Your cluster: _____

Expanding What You Have Learned

You will learn more about goal management and your strengths and weaknesses through logging than by any other means.

1. Start at least one log now.

2. After you have completed your first 14-day logs, record here what you learned:
   About yourself as a goal manager:

   _____
   _____

   About your goals:

   _____
   _____

   About the theory and practice of goal management:

   _____
   _____

3. How does goal management use the three principles of Total Quality Management?
   Measure: _____
   Improve: _____
   Communicate: _____

Chapter 6 Checkpoints

✓ Step 1 to goal success: Commit yourself to developing new goal-achieving habits.

✓ Step 2 to goal success: Measure your practice of new habits until you have new habits of success.

✓ Concentrate on goals that are realistic and achievable.

✓ Review *all* logs daily, even though you may not be working on them until tomorrow.

✓ If your logs get interrupted identify blocks. Consider designing "habit clusters" and new rewards.

7 | Combining Work and Exercise

This chapter will help you to:

- Productively combine goal tasks and planning with exercise.
- Improve your health and increase your energy and stamina to meet your goals.

OVERCOMING BARRIERS

Goal management provides many strategies for overcoming barriers to achieving goals. You have already seen how to use daily record-keeping to document your progress, how to eliminate chronic time wasters, how to set priorities, and how to improve your techniques. This chapter describes two additional strategies for success: keeping fit and combining tasks with exercise.

EXERCISE AND EXCELLENCE

In his book *Fit for Success*, James Rippe, M.D., summarized his 1989 study of 1,139 CEOs and senior managers: "The message was always the same. It was a message of linkage: the link between their health and fitness practices and their high level of performance."

Like Dr. Rippe's CEOs, we all know that regular exercise has many benefits. It increases your energy and stamina, helps you control your weight, decreases risk of heart disease and cancer, improves moods, lengthens life, and reducing stress. Good health and exercise habits have always been considered necessary for successful time and stress management. Thus, fitness and time management are *linked to achieving your goals*:

Figure 7.1   Synergy at work

THE MAGIC OF SYNERGY

Despite the benefits of exercise, 70 to 80 percent of all persons who begin exercise routines quit within three months. Only 23 percent of Americans exercise regularly. Why? The reasons include boredom, lack of time, inconvenience, or lack of support. These same disappointing results apply to the practice of time management.

How can you beat these odds? A proven way is to *combine tasks*. Everyone sometimes does two things at once. You might exercise or sew while watching the news, or catch up on family happenings while preparing a meal. Of course, the strategy can be a time waster if you try to combine the wrong tasks, such as typing while you are talking on the phone. But combining well-planned, well-paired tasks creates *synergy*. In other words, it creates a "sum-is-greater-than-its-parts" effect. How does this occur?

- Combining routines creates interesting tasks, eliminating boredom.
- Combining tasks saves time.
- Combining routines, such as exercise and planning, gives you two motivating options. On a day that you don't feel like performing one task, your motivation to perform the other task gets you started, and vice versa. (Chapter 6 habit clusters are effective in habit formation because they utilize this principle.)
- As you perform tasks together, you'll get better at *both* tasks, and your motivation will rise.

COMBINING FITNESS AND GOAL MANAGEMENT

Combining exercise with tasks brings a special benefit. When you perform aerobic exercise, oxygen and endorphins (natural painkillers) pour into your bloodstream. They lessen pain, raise your mood, and improve your mental functioning. Your mental productivity increases. Thus, when you combine exercise and goal management, you put to work a *goal-management equation for excellence*, which is based on economic theory:

1 Unit of Exercise + 1 Unit of Goal Management = 3 Productive Units

This chapter shows three ways to put this equation into practice.

Stretching and Evaluating

The most common exercises are warm-up and cool-down stretches, which should always come before and after vigorous exercise or work. Figure 7.2 "Stretching for Your Goals" shows how you can link stretching with thinking about goal management. It gives a stretching exercise for eight parts of the body and a corresponding goal management question.

For each stretch complete these steps:

1. Inhale at the stretch and touch the specified part of the body while saying its corresponding statement.
2. Hold the stretch for 10 seconds while you answer its corresponding goal-management question.
3. Release the stretch and exhale relaxing the muscles.
4. Repeat Steps 1–3 at least three times before going on to the next part of the body.
5. Perform all eight stretches, Steps 1–4, to complete one set.

For a 5- to 10-minute warm-up or cool-down, do one to three sets of stretches. During and after sets, record new insights, answers, or future tasks on the appropriate goal-management worksheet.

7

Questions

1. Goals

As you touch your neck and breathe in get ready to think about your goals.

As you hold your stretch ask yourself:

"Which image, skill, or habit goal needs review and development today?"

2. Goal Tasks

As you touch your shoulders and breathe in, get ready to think about today's goal/task.

As you hold your stretch ask yourself:

"What specific 15-minute goal tasks can I do today to get closer to achieving this goal?"

3. Support Systems

As you touch your arms and breathe in, get ready to think about your support systems.

As you hold your stretch ask yourself:

"Do I let myself, my co-workers, and the people I care for talk about and encourage my attempts to achieve my goals?"

4. Information Processing

As you touch your back and breathe in, get ready to think about how you process information.

As you hold your stretch ask yourself:

"Am I processing my goal-task information efficiently?"

Exercise

1. Neck

Pull head gently to your chest, then to each side, but not back.

2. Shoulders

Shrug shoulders front, up, backs, and down.

3. Arms

Clasp your hands behind you. With your right arm up, stretch. With your left arm up, stretch. Stretch up with both arms.

4. Back

Imagine you are holding a big beach ball. Push it hard against your stomach.

Figure 7.2   Stretching For Your Goals

Questions

5. Goal-Time Wasters

As you touch your stomach and breathe in, get ready to think about your goal-time wasters.

As you hold your stretch ask yourself:

"How are my goal-time wasters preventing me from completing my goal tasks? How are the goal-time wasters of my friends, co-workers, or loved ones preventing me from completing my goal tasks?"

6. Goal–Time-Management Talk

As you touch your waist and breathe in, get ready to think about your goal–time-management talk.

As you hold your stretch ask yourself:

"Do I use goal–time-management words when I talk to myself or others, or do I use the self-defeating words of people who resist goal-achievement in their lives and mine?"

7. Daily Planning

As you touch your legs get ready to think about your daily planning.

As you hold your stretch ask yourself:

"Am I planning my goal tasks and working my goal business plans?"

8. Personal Organization

As you stretch your feet, get ready to think about your systems of organization.

As you hold your stretch ask yourself:

"Is personal disorganization preventing me or my helpers from completing my goal tasks?"

Exercise

5. Stomach

Pull your head and chest up and hold the position.

6. Waist

Reach to each side.

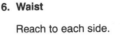

7. Legs

Stretch each calf.

8. Feet

Tense and release each foot, curling your toe forward.

Figure 7.2   *(continued)*

Using a Stationary Bike

A great combination of exercise and goal management is to use a stationary bike with a drafting table placed over for writing. (A movable hospital tray, found in medical supply stores, works well also, though it has a smaller working surface. Using a Stair Master™ with a plastic reading stand will also work.)

Combine exercise and planning to get new insights on tricky problems. Don't waste this time reading the newspaper or writing today's to-do list. Instead, use this time to step back, evaluate, find out what is troubling you, or get that missing solution to your latest management problem. Then, let your clearer, keener mind generate its best insights and solutions of the day.

Problem-Solving Walks and Runs

You can solve problems while you walk or run if you:

1. Decide ahead what specific problem you want to solve.
2. Use a short problem-solving system, on paper or in your memory, to organize your thoughts, rather than just ruminating on the problem. (See page 10 for a problem-solving model.)
3. Pause to record insights as you walk or run "through your problem."

Expanding What You Have Learned

Look again at Figure 7.2. How would you adapt the questions in the figure to other exercises, such as weight training, aerobics, running, and rowing?

_____

_____

_____

Chapter 7 Checkpoints

✓ Combining goal tasks is the easiest way to "make time" and improve your productivity.

✓ Exercise always improves your performance and mood.

✓ Memorize the stretching exercises shown. They can be easily recalled because they move naturally from top to bottom:

- neck
- shoulders
- arms
- back
- stomach
- waist
- legs
- feet

8 | Boosting Your Goal-Management Skills

This chapter will help you to:

- Support your new goal-management skills and habits through:

    Positive self-talk.

    Organized workspaces.

    Reminders and cues.

    Mentors and partners.

    New structures.

- Identify your strengths and weaknesses as a goal manager.

CREATING SUPPORT SYSTEMS

Old habits die hard, and, as we have noted, new ones take at least one month of daily practice to create. Now we must examine ways to ensure that your skills, habits, and goal-management systems will be used, enhanced, and maintained in the years to come.

If we look at people who have achieved their goals, we find that they have addressed this problem by creating *support systems* to remind them of their goals, to stay on course, and to overcome distractions. Here are some basic systems to ensure your long-term success as a goal manager.

Self-Talk: Friend or Foe?

Most people spend about five hours each day mentally talking to themselves *about themselves*. Since we all speak to ourselves at an average rate of 200 words per minute, you say about 60,000 words to yourself during your five hours of daily self-talk.

You have self-talk phrases for every aspect of your life: your self-image, your body image, your intelligence, your insecurities, your past, your job, your social life, your future, and so on. Each group of self-talk phrases affects some aspect of your goal-achievement potential. Is your self-talk helping or hurting your attempts to master your goals? Discover your self-talk by completing this self-talk script. If you discover difficult issues you cannot explain, consider consulting appropriate texts or professionals.

8

List phrases you say to yourself about your life:

Job   Social Life   Future

_____   _____   _____
_____   _____   _____
_____   _____   _____
_____   _____   _____

Other Area _____   Other Area _____   Other Area _____

_____   _____   _____
_____   _____   _____
_____   _____   _____
_____   _____   _____

Create new self-talk scripts. List new goal-supporting self-talk phrases you could use:

Job   Social Life   Future

_____   _____   _____
_____   _____   _____
_____   _____   _____
_____   _____   _____

Other Area _____   Other Area _____   Other Area _____

_____   _____   _____
_____   _____   _____
_____   _____   _____
_____   _____   _____

Workspaces and Organization

All of your present living spaces and workspaces are associated with your current habits. These spaces reinforce the very behaviors that may hold you back. If you want to commit yourself to new goals, you should change as many of your environments as possible.

- *Make it new.* When you walk into your office or study, does it "say" anything to you? Probably not. But if you rearrange the room with art, signs, and new furniture, you will know you're somewhere new as soon as you enter the room. Rename rooms as goal rooms, such as your "Exercise Room," "Writing Room," and so on. The room itself will remind you that you are putting aside your old ways and working on new goal-achieving skills and habits.
- *Make it neat and pleasant.* Your environment should inspire you to excellence. Remember that disorder encourages procrastination.

Reminders and Cues

Most people post reminders around the house and office. But, after a week, they just blend in. For these "external memories" to help you, you need to design them with care and creativity:

1. Move your posted reminders every week, preferably to places where they get in the way and you have to handle them.
2. Make signs for your desk, table corners, and mirrors that refer to your current goals and their targets.
3. Every time you bring a new article of clothing, art work, appliance, or object into the house or office, associate it with one of your goals. You might have "a lose-weight watch," "a write-a-book scarf," "an exercise rubber tree." The association of two seemingly odd objects is the world's oldest memory technique.
4. Carry your goal-management worksheets with you. They are your most valuable reminders.

8

Mentors and Partners

What do Big Brother and Big Sister organizations, Weight Watchers, AA, and apprenticeship programs all have in common? They all use "buddy systems" or mentors. You may recall that Worksheet 4 shows that a key stage of all of your goals is creating support systems and that you should design your goal business plans to include the invaluable assistance of a mentor or partner. Mentors and partners make your efforts more enjoyable, stimulating, and successful for one simple reason: You meet deadlines and your own expectations more often with them than without them.

Be aware of the difference between mentors and partners:

- *Mentors.* Mentors can provide wise, unbiased management advice and career direction and can help design a goal business plan, including project Worksheet 5. Most friends, coworkers, and family won't work well as mentors because they too easily accept—and often legitimate—your procrastination. Unless they offer, never ask mentors to become active partners in your goal projects. Most potential mentors are so successful that they are too busy to start a new project.
- *Partners.* Partnerships can be informal or formal, short or long term. Unlike mentors, partners are *working* members of your goal projects. In any of these forms, a partnership provides motivation, commitment, and a structure that provides discipline.

Think About It

Mentors and partners have made a difference. To remind you of the importance of mentors and partners, recall past business and personal projects or decisions you made with the help of a mentor and/or partner.

Decision or Project	Mentor's Name	Partner's Name
_____	_____	_____
_____	_____	_____
_____	_____	_____
_____	_____	_____

Creating New "Structures"

What structures in our society keep people on track with their goals? You might think of educational courses, formal degree or certification programs, regular sessions with physical or mental therapists, and support groups such as Weight Watchers or AA. This is not a long list.

At the same time the world is overflowing with distractions. Creating a *very visible structure* is the best way to combat distractions. To create structures that will support your goals:

- Enroll in a course that will create an outcome related to your goals. For example, your course work could serve as research for a goal, or it might teach you a skill required by an image goal.
- Create a support group that meets regularly. It might consist of people who want to master a skill you can teach or people who will serve as your "informal board of directors," reviewing your performance on goal tasks.
- Be disciplined about working on goal tasks and habits during block times. For example, always write from 6:30 to 7:30 AM, or always exercise while watching the evening news.
- Above all, *use* your daily planners and habit logs—keep them out and visible.

Putting It All Together

To design a support system:

1. Select an image, skill, or habit goal you want to start working on next week.
2. Fill out Worksheet 4 for that goal.
3. Treat Stage III, "Create Support Systems," as a project and complete Worksheet 5 for this project.

ASSESS YOUR STRENGTHS AND WEAKNESSES

Take another look at your strengths and weaknesses as a goal manager by completing Post-Test on page 95. Compare your score with the one you received on the Self-Assessment. How are you doing? To maintain your gains, regularly review this text, Worksheets 1 through 10, and the Skill Maintenance checklist inside the back cover.

Chapter 8 Checkpoints

✓ Are you controlling your self-talk that relates to your goal-management abilities and targets?

✓ Are your workplaces organized and motivating for successful goal management?

✓ Have you surrounded yourself with positive goal reminders and cues?

✓ Who will you ask to be your mentors or partners? Remember, they need a reason for helping you.

✓ What structures have you created to keep you on track and on time in meeting your targets?

✓ To keep yourself motivated and focused, review Worksheets 1 through 10 each week.

Post-Test

Analyze your strengths and weaknesses as a goal manager. Read each statement and mark the appropriate space.

	Almost Always	Some-times	Almost Never
1. I can recite from memory my three top goals.	_____	_____	_____
2. I know what my most important needs are.	_____	_____	_____
3. Every time I complete a difficult task, I reward myself.	_____	_____	_____
4. I pursue goals for which I am not properly prepared.	_____	_____	_____
5. I have daily routines for each major goal.	_____	_____	_____
6. When I have important projects, I write a project plan.	_____	_____	_____
7. Establishing new work habits is easy for me.	_____	_____	_____
8. I consider myself a good manager of time.	_____	_____	_____
9. I regularly do things to reduce my stress.	_____	_____	_____
10. I set realistic goals for myself.	_____	_____	_____
11. When I begin a skill or habit, I measure my progress.	_____	_____	_____
12. I use success words when I talk to myself.	_____	_____	_____
13. I use success words when I talk to other people.	_____	_____	_____
14. I plan my work each day on paper.	_____	_____	_____
15. My work and home spaces are well organized.	_____	_____	_____
16. I can easily find what I need in the office files.	_____	_____	_____
17. My friends and family actively support my goals.	_____	_____	_____

18. The people I work with support my
goals.   _____ _____ _____

19. I exercise vigorously three times a week. _____ _____ _____

20. I feel that I am getting what I want out of
life.   _____ _____ _____

     Totals   _____ _____ _____

For every check of *Almost Always*, give yourself two points.

For every check of *Sometimes*, give yourself one point.

For every check of *Almost Never*, give yourself no points.

Add up each column for your total score.

How does this score compare with your score on the Self-Assessment checklist? See page 1 to interpret your score.

Business Skills Express Series

This growing series of books addresses a broad range of key business skills and topics to meet the needs of employees, human resource departments, and training consultants.

To obtain information about these and other Business Skills Express books, please call Irwin Professional Publishing toll free at: 1-800-634-3966.

Effective Performance Management
ISBN   1-55623-867-3

Hiring the Best
ISBN   1-55623-865-7

Writing that Works
ISBN   1-55623-856-8

Customer Service Excellence
ISBN   1-55623-969-6

Writing for Business Results
ISBN   1-55623-854-1

Powerful Presentation Skills
ISBN   1-55623-870-3

Meetings That Work
ISBN   1-55623-866-5

Effective Teamwork
ISBN   1-55623-880-0

Time Management
ISBN   1-55623-888-6

Assertiveness Skills
ISBN   1-55623-857-6

Motivation at Work
ISBN   1-55623-868-1

Overcoming Anxiety at Work
ISBN   1-55623-869-X

Positive Politics at Work
ISBN   1-55623-879-7

Telephone Skills at Work
ISBN   1-55623-858-4

Managing Conflict at Work
ISBN   1-55623-890-8

The New Supervisor: Skills for Success
ISBN   1-55623-762-6

The Americans with Disabilities Act: What Supervisors Need to Know
ISBN   1-55623-889-4

Managing the Demands of Work and Home
ISBN   0-7863-0221-6

Effective Listening Skills
ISBN   0-7863-0102-4

Goal Management at Work
ISBN   0-7863-0225-9

Positive Attitudes at Work
ISBN   0-7863-0100-8

Supervising the Difficult Employee
ISBN   0-7863-0219-4

Cultural Diversity in the Workplace
ISBN   0-7863-0125-2

Managing Organizational Change
ISBN   0-7863-0162-7

Negotiating for Business Results
ISBN   0-7863-0114-7

Practical Business Communication
ISBN   0-7863-0227-5

High Performance Speaking
ISBN   0-7863-0222-4

Delegation Skills
ISBN   0-7863-0105-9

Coaching Skills: A Guide for Supervisors
ISBN   0-7863-0220-8

Customer Service and the Telephone
ISBN   0-7863-0224-0

Creativity at Work
ISBN   0-7863-0223-2

Effective Interpersonal Relationships
ISBN   0-7863-0255-0

The Participative Leader
ISBN   0-7863-0252-6

Building Customer Loyalty
ISBN   0-7863-0253-4

Getting and Staying Organized
ISBN   0-7863-0254-2

Total Quality Selling
ISBN   0-7863-0324-7

Business Etiquette
ISBN   0-7863-0323-9

Empowering Employees
ISBN   0-7863-0309-3

Training Skills for Supervisors
ISBN   0-7863-0308-5